GUIDELINES

SUCCOS

GUIDELINES

Over Four Hundred
of the Most Commonly
Asked Questions about
SUCCOS

Rabbi Elozor Barclay
Rabbi Yitzchok Jaeger

TARGUM/FELDHEIM

First published 2002

Copyright © 2002 by E. Barclay & Y. Jaeger

ISBN 1-56871-205-7

Please address any questions or comments
regarding these books to the authors:
E. Barclay (02) 583 0914
Y. Jaeger (02) 583 4889
email: jaeger@barak-online.net

By the same authors:
GUIDELINES TO PESACH
GUIDELINES TO THE YOMIM NORAIM
GUIDELINES TO CHANUKAH
GUIDELINES TO PURIM

Please contact the authors for details regarding
dedication opportunities for future volumes.

Published by:
Targum Press, Inc.
22700 W. Eleven Mile Rd.
Southfield, MI 48034
E-mail: targum@netvision.net.il
Fax toll free: (888) 298-9992

Distributed by:
Feldheim Publishers
200 Airport Executive Park
Nanuet, NY 10954
www.feldheim.com

Printed in Israel

הרב רפאל צבי ובר

רב דקהילת קמניץ

ונוה יעקב מזרח, ירושלים

ט' תמוז תשס"ב

בס"ד

מכתב ברכה

שמחתי לראות קונטרס הלכות בשפה
האנגלית שיצא לאור ע״י ידידי הרב ר'
אלעזר ברקלי שליט״א והרב ר' יצחק ייגר
שליט״א, והנני מכירם ויודעם בהשתדלות
לאסוקי שמעתתא אליבא דהלכתא.

והנני מברכם שיקבלו דבריהם בביהמ״ד.

בברכת התורה,

צבי ובר

Rabbi Nachman Bulman
Yeshivat Ohr Somayach
Beit Knesset Nachliel

רב נחמן בולמן

מנהל רוחני ישיבת אור שמח
רב ק"ק נחליאל נוה יעקב מזרח

בע"ה

יום ו', י"ח תמוז, תשס"ב פה עיה"ק ת"ו

Friday, eighteenth of Tammuz, 5762, the holy city of Yerushalayim.

I was delighted to see the fifth volume of the **Guidelines** series. The questions and answers in **Guidelines** provide a clear and easily understood format and clarify relevant halachic issues.

It is clear from the quality of this work that Rabbi Elozor Barclay and Rabbi Yitzchok Jaeger have invested great amounts of time and effort in their thorough investigation of these dinim. Every answer has been written carefully and thoughtfully, considering both the classic and the most up-to-date halachic authorities. The accurate Hebrew references will certainly be an invaluable aid for any reader who wishes to investigate further.

I highly recommend this book to any person who is truly searching to know the correct conduct.

Signed with admiration,

נחמן בולמן

מנהל רוחני ישיבת אור שמח
רב ק"ק נחליאל נוה יעקב מזרח ביום הנ"ל
ועיני נשואות לשמים להסכמת שוכן במרומים

RABBI ZEV LEFF
Rabbi of Moshav Matisyahu
Rosh Hayeshiva Yeshiva Gedola Matisyahu

בס"ד

כ"ב סיון תשס"ב

It is with great pleasure that I have received the latest addition to the series of Halachic Guides produced by Rabbi Elozor Barclay שליט"א and Rabbi Yitzchok Jaeger שליט"א - **Guidelines** to Succos.

This is an impressive work which will serve as an invaluable aid to those who seek to be guided through this important period of the Jewish year.

As in the previous volumes the laws are lucidly and concisely presented in a manner that will serve as a guide and source for the beginner and a source of review for the advanced student. I highly recommend this work as all the other volumes of this series.

May Hashem grant the authors long life and health and ability to continue to merit Klal Yisroel with the promulgation of Torah and mitzvos.

With Torah blessings,

Rabbi Zev Leff

Table of Contents

Foreword

With praise and gratitude to Hashem we present a basic guide to the laws of Succos. Our books on the laws of Pesach, the Yomim Noraim, Chanukah and Purim were warmly received by the public, encouraging and motivating us to develop this fifth volume.

Rarely will a written work be a perfect substitute for a one-to-one discussion with a rav. The answer to a query often depends upon various factors that only further questioning can clarify. Even though much thought and effort has been invested in the phrasing and wording used, it is possible that *halachos* may be incorrectly applied or misunderstood. Accordingly, any doubts that arise should be discussed with one's local rav.

Our primary intent is to guide the reader through the maze of laws and customs that abound during these joyous days, hence the title GUIDELINES. The laws of Succos are numerous and complex and a person who is not familiar with them will certainly not be able to fulfill his obligation properly.

We would like to express our thanks to the *halachic* authorities who assisted in the preparation of this work. Two exceptional *Talmidei Chachomim* graciously took time from their busy schedules to help turn this book into a reality. Rav Yirmiyahu Kaganoff, *shlita*, thoroughly checked the entire manuscript, providing many invaluable comments and observations. Rav Yitzchok Kaufman, *shlita*, a renowned expert in the laws of the four species, read through the entire text and made numerous valuable corrections and suggestions.

Thanks are also due to Rabbi Moshe Dombey and all the staff at Targum Press who have once again demonstrated their professional expertise with the production of this book.

It is our hope that in the merit of keeping the laws of Succos punctiliously, we will be worthy to sit in the succah reserved for the righteous in the world to come.

Elozor Barclay   Yitzchok Jaeger

Yerushalayim, Tammuz 5762

Chapter One
Building the Succah

1. When should one begin building the succah?

According to most opinions, one should begin on *motzai* Yom Kippur in order to go immediately from one mitzvah to another. If this is not possible, he should begin the following morning. If this will not leave him sufficient time to complete the succah, he may begin to build before Yom Kippur, but he should not place the *s'chach* until after Yom Kippur. According to some opinions, one should begin to build the succah before Yom Kippur, as an added merit.

2. When should one finish the construction?

Ideally, the succah should be completed on the day after Yom Kippur. However, if by doing so, the succah will not be built properly and sturdily, he should devote more time to erect a better and more beautiful succah.

3. May one build the succah on *erev* Shabbos or *erev* Yom Tov?

Yes, but one must stop building at *halachic* midday. According to some opinions, one may continue to build until *mincha ketanah* (two-and-a-half *halachic* hours before sunset).

4. May one build a succah on *chol hamoed*?

If a person did not build a succah before Yom Tov, or if he built one but it fell down, he may build one on *chol hamoed*. If necessary, even skilled work (which is usually forbidden on *chol hamoed*) is permitted in order to fulfill the mitzvah, but if possible this type of work should be avoided and the succah should be a simple construction.

5. Is anyone allowed to build a succah?

Any person may build a succah, including women and children. However, it is a mitzvah for every man to participate personally in the building, and whoever toils and sweats with this task receives atonement for serious sins. It is preferable not to ask a gentile to build a succah (see question 220).

6. Is everyone qualified to put on the *s'chach*?

Ideally, the *s'chach* should be put on by a Jewish man. If the *s'chach* was put on by a woman, child or gentile, the succah is kosher. According to some opinions, such *s'chach* should be raised and lowered by a Jewish man.

7. May one build a succah anywhere?

A succah must be built under the sky, with nothing intervening between the *s'chach* and the sky. One must be careful not to build a succah under:

- A roof (see also question 53).
- An overhanging balcony.
- A tree.
- Protruding *s'chach* of another succah.

8. What if one part of the succah is under the sky and one part is not?

If the section under the sky has sufficient walls and the minimum dimensions (see chapter two), the succah is kosher. Nevertheless, a man may only eat in the part of the succah that is under the sky. Sometimes, the invalid section may be included in calculating the size of the succah and a rav should be consulted.

9. May the succah be built near a tree if the branches sway over the *s'chach* in the wind?

Ideally, one should chop off these branches. If one did not do so, the succah is still kosher even when the branches are swaying over the *s'chach*.

10. May one build a succah underneath washing lines?

Yes. Since the lines are very narrow and there is space between them, they do not invalidate the succah. This is true even when laundry is hanging from the lines. However, if the laundry becomes entangled in the lines, the area of the *s'chach* beneath is invalidated. In some situations, this may invalidate the entire succah.

11. May one build a succah in a public area?

• In *Eretz Yisrael*, this is allowed since permission is automatically granted to use the street for this purpose.

• In *chutz la'aretz*, one should ideally avoid doing this unless specific permission is obtained from the authorities. However, the custom is to be lenient in this matter if no other area is available, especially if the succah is built close to the house.

12. May one build a succah in a communal yard?

Since each person has a share in the yard, he is allowed to build a succah there. However, he should not build it in a place that will cause an obstruction or any other inconvenience to neighbors without prior permission.

13. May a person build a succah near garbage?

This is permitted if no foul smell reaches the succah.

14. May one build a succah near sewage pipes?

This is permitted if the pipes are closed and no foul smell is emitted.

15. May one build a succah on soil?

This is permitted, but it is forbidden to sweep the floor on Shabbos and Yom Tov. It is therefore advisable to cover the floor with some suitable flooring.

16. May one build a succah on grass?

This is not advisable since it is difficult to avoid spilling liquids on the grass on Shabbos and Yom Tov. The grass should be covered with suitable flooring.

17. May one build a succah in a place where he is afraid to sleep?

See question 90.

18. Does the succah require a *mezuzah*?

Since the succah is only a temporary dwelling, it does not require a *mezuzah*.

Chapter Two

The Succah

Note: The figures given in this chapter are approximate. When the measurements of one's succah are very close to these figures, a rav should be consulted.

19. What is the minimum size of the succah?

The inside of the succah must measure at least seven *tefachim* long by seven *tefachim* wide. This is the smallest area in which a person could reasonably be expected to sit. In practice, this means that the succah should preferably measure 70cm x 70cm. It is still kosher if it measures only 56cm x 56cm.

20. May the succah be long and narrow?

Even if the succah is very long, it must still measure at least seven *tefachim* wide.

21. May a low balcony wall be included in the width?

Some narrow balconies lack the required width in the floor measurement but meet the requirement when including the width of the wall. A succah built on such a balcony is kosher provided that:

- The wall is less than 80cm high.
- The *s'chach* is at least 80cm higher than the wall (preferably 1m).

22. What is the required measurement of a different shaped succah (circular, triangular etc)?

The succah must be large enough to contain a square measuring seven by seven *tefachim*.

23. What is the maximum size of the succah?

There is no limit to the size of the succah.

24. What is the minimum height of the succah?

Preferably the internal height should measure at least 1m, but it is still kosher if it measures only 80cm.

25. What if pieces of *s'chach* hang down into this space?

This should be avoided since it may invalidate the succah.

26. What if decorations hang down into this space?

The succah is still kosher (see also question 61).

27. What is the maximum height of the succah?

The *s'chach* must not be higher than twenty *amos* from the floor of the succah (approx. ten meters). This is rarely applicable.

28.   How many walls should a succah have?

Strictly speaking, a succah may be kosher even if it has less than three complete walls. However, the custom is to build a succah with four complete walls to avoid complications. In order of preference, a succah should have:

- Four complete walls.
- Three complete walls.
- Four incomplete walls.
- Three incomplete walls.

A succah that does not have complete walls should be checked by a rav to ascertain if it is kosher.

29.   From which materials should the walls be made?

The walls may be made from any sturdy material.

30.   May sheets be used for the walls?

The walls must be strong enough to remain in position when the wind blows. Therefore, sheets that flap may not be used. Ideally, one should not even use sheets that are firmly tied down on all sides, in case they become detached and this goes unnoticed. If three walls are made from sturdy materials, one may use sheets for the fourth wall.

31.   May one use sheets in extenuating circumstances?

If no alternatives are available, one may use sheets that are tied down on all sides. In this situation, it is preferable to tie several horizontal strings around the succah. These strings should be tied at intervals of less than 24cm, to a height of at least 80cm (preferably to a height of 1m). This method invokes a *halachic* principle that considers the strings to be united to form a solid wall. With such strings, the succah is kosher according to all opinions.

32.   How high must the walls be?

The walls must be at least 80cm high (preferably 1m) but do not need to reach the *s'chach*. It is perfectly acceptable to support the *s'chach* on wooden posts etc, if the walls are the minimum height. The remaining spaces may be left open or filled with sheets or any other material. In this situation, the *s'chach* should preferably reach the line directly above the wall. (See question 45 about the *s'chach* reaching the walls in the horizontal direction.)

33.   Must the walls touch the ground?

The walls do not need to touch the ground, but they must not be raised more than 24cm above it.

Chapter Three
The S'chach

34. Which materials may be used for *s'chach*?

The Torah requires one to use a material that satisfies these three conditions:

- It is vegetation.
- It is detached from the ground.
- It is incapable of becoming *tamei*.

However, there are other conditions added by the Sages that disqualify certain types of *s'chach* (see questions 36, 38 and 39).

35. Is there a preferred material for *s'chach*?

According to one opinion, the best *s'chach* is cut branches of trees. This is hinted by the numerical value of the word succah (סוכה - 91) which is identical to that of the word tree ('ilan' - אילן).

36. Are all branches suitable?

Most are kosher, but one should not use the following types:

- Branches whose leaves tend to shrivel, since it is difficult to estimate how much *s'chach* is required.
- Branches whose leaves tend to fall off into the succah.
- Those that have an unpleasant smell.

- Those that are liable to contain flies or bugs that may fall into the succah.

37. May one cut branches from trees in the street or countryside?

It is forbidden to fulfill a mitzvah through stealing. Therefore, permission must be obtained before cutting any such trees, unless one is certain that they are ownerless.

38. May one use planks of wood for *s'chach*?

It is forbidden to use wide planks for *s'chach*, since the succah would then appear like a house. Therefore, one may not use planks that are wider than 8cm, and preferably not wider than 5cm. Narrow planks may be used, although they are disqualified by some opinions.

39. May one use narrow planks sawn from wooden objects such as crates, boxes, tables, closets etc?

Many wooden objects are disqualified since they are capable of becoming *tamei*, and even after they are broken they may still not be used. When they have been destroyed beyond recognition, e.g. after being sawn up into planks, there is still a difference of opinions whether they are suitable. However, all opinions permit the use of planks made from very large crates (approx. 20 cubic feet) since they were never capable of becoming *tamei*.

40.   May one use matting, wickerwork etc.?

When pieces of *s'chach* are interwoven or connected to each other, they may be disqualified since they now may be capable of becoming *tamei*. Since these laws are complex, one should not use such matting or wickerwork unless it has a reliable *hechsher*.

41.   How much *s'chach* must be used?

One must use sufficient *s'chach* to cover the majority of the area of the roof. In other words, the total area of the open spaces must be less than the area covered.

42.   What if the *s'chach* is dense in some areas but sparse in others?

The succah is kosher if the following two conditions are fulfilled:
- The total area covered by *s'chach* is the majority of the succah (see previous question).
- The densely covered area exceeds the sparsely covered area.

43.   May one sit under a sparsely covered area?

Yes, unless the area measures seven by seven *tefachim* (see question 19). It is advisable to spread the *s'chach* evenly, so that every part of the succah is covered sufficiently.

44.   May one cover the succah with very dense *s'chach*?

There are several levels of kashrus:

- Ideally, there should be sufficient spaces in the *s'chach* that one will be able to see some stars at night.
- If not, there should be a few spaces that will allow in a little sunlight during the day.
- Even if there are no spaces at all the succah is still kosher. One may be lenient to do this in cold or windy places, where a person may be tempted to leave the succah if there is insufficient *s'chach*.
- If the *s'chach* is so dense that even rain cannot penetrate, the succah is invalid according to some opinions, since it resembles a house.

45.   Must the *s'chach* extend horizontally up to the walls?

No, but the *s'chach* must reach within 24cm of the walls. Nevertheless, one must not sit next to the wall under the empty space, unless it is less than 20cm.

46.   What if the space between the *s'chach* and the wall is more than 24cm?

Then the wall next to the space is invalid and cannot be used as one of the three minimum walls. If the *s'chach* reaches the other three walls then the succah is kosher, but if two walls are invalidated then the entire succah is invalid.

47.   Is there any way to correct such a situation?

Yes. If there are large gaps (more than 24cm) between the *s'chach* and the walls, one should fill them in. Sheets, metal, boards or anything else may be used, although these items may not be used as *s'chach*. This method invokes a halachic principle called *dofen akumah* - a bent wall. We imagine that the wall of the succah extends upwards and then bends in horizontally until it reaches the kosher *s'chach*. One may not sit under this area of the succah, but only under the kosher *s'chach*.

48. Is there any limitation to this method?

This method is permitted provided that:

- The non-kosher *s'chach* is less than 1.92m wide on at least three sides **and**
- The area of kosher *s'chach* is at least seven by seven *tefachim*.

This situation is common when making a succah indoors under a removable section of the ceiling.

49. May one place the *s'chach* on a metal frame?

This should be avoided. Just as the *s'chach* itself must not be capable of becoming *tamei*, similarly the supports of the *s'chach* should not be capable of becoming *tamei*. Therefore, the *s'chach* should preferably be placed on wooded beams. In extenuating circumstances, one may use anything as supports for the *s'chach*. Similarly, if one visits a succah whose *s'chach* rests on a metal frame, one may eat there and recite the *b'racha* for the succah.

50. What if the wooden support beams rest on a metal frame?

This is permitted since the metal frame is only a secondary support to the primary wooden supports. According to some opinions, this is true only if the wooden beams are actually assisting in the support of the *s'chach* (i.e. the removal of the wooden beams would cause the *s'chach* to fall down). If after removing the wooden beams the *s'chach* would still rest on the metal frame, the metal frame is considered to be the primary support according to this opinion.

51. May one tie or nail the *s'chach* to the wooden supports?

One should avoid using string or nails to support the *s'chach*. If a person is afraid that the *s'chach* may slide off or be blown away in a normal wind, he should not tie or nail it down since this is considered a primary support. Rather, he should place heavy planks of wood (see question 38) or branches over the *s'chach*, since they qualify as kosher *s'chach*. The planks or branches may be tied or nailed down since the string or nails would then be considered a secondary support. Alternatively, he may tie down the *s'chach* with vegetation, such as palm leaves, twigs etc. If the *s'chach* would not be blown away except in an unusually strong wind, it may be tied down even with string. In extenuating circumstances, the *s'chach* may be tied down with string, even if it may blow away in a normal wind (see question 49).

52. Must the walls be built before the s'chach?

Yes, the walls must be constructed before the s'chach is put in place. If the s'chach is placed on a frame and then the walls built, the succah is invalid and the s'chach should be raised and lowered. Similarly, if one needs to use the 'bent wall' method, the 'bent wall' must be constructed before the s'chach is placed.

53. May one build the succah under a roof and then remove the roof?

If the s'chach is placed on the succah before the roof is removed then:

- If the roof is part of the permanent building, the succah is kosher.
- If the roof is designed to open and close, the succah is not kosher. In this case, the roof must be opened before the s'chach is placed on the succah. If the s'chach was placed on the succah before the roof was opened, the roof should be opened and then each piece of s'chach raised and lowered.

54. May the roof be closed after the s'chach has been correctly placed?

Yes, but it is praiseworthy to re-open it just before Yom Tov commences. It is certainly permitted to close and re-open the roof after Yom Tov has begun (see question 154).

55.   Who is qualified to place the *s'chach* on the succah?

See question 6.

56.   What should one think about when placing the *s'chach*?

One should think that the *s'chach* is being placed in order:

- to provide shade or
- to fulfill the mitzvah of succah.

Chapter Four

Decorating the Succah

57. Should one decorate the succah?

All mitzvah objects should be made beautiful, and especially the succah. Just as a person decorates and beautifies his home, so too should he decorate his succah which is his home for the week of Succos. The more a person embellishes the succah, the more he is to be praised.

58. How should one decorate the succah?

The walls should be covered with decorative sheets or drapes, and fruits should be hung from the roof. It is a widespread custom to hang pictures on the walls and any other means may be used to add joy and pleasure when sitting in the succah. According to one opinion, the use of paper chains etc. is questionable since people do not usually hang them in their homes.

59. May one use decorations made by gentiles?

It is permitted to use such decorations, even though the gentiles may have intended them to be used for their own holidays. Some opinions question their use, and a person should use his own judgement and sensitivity.

60. May one write verses to decorate the succah?

Some opinions criticize this practice since the paper on which the verses are written may subsequently not be treated with proper respect. Nevertheless, the widespread custom is to allow this and care should be taken to avoid disrespect. (Old or torn decorations containing verses must be buried with *sheimos*. See question 206.)

61. How low may the decorations hang?

A person does not fulfill the mitzvah when sitting underneath an object that is 4 *tefachim* wide and 4 *tefachim* from the *s'chach*. Therefore, as a precaution, all decorations should be hung within 32cm of the *s'chach* even if they are narrow. If the *s'chach* is low, one must be careful to hang the decorations sufficiently high that they are out of reach of young children, who may be tempted to detach them on Shabbos and Yom Tov.

62. What if the decorations begin within 32cm but descend below that height?

This should be avoided if possible.

63. What if branches of *s'chach* descend below 32cm?

This is permitted. However, the succah is enhanced if the *s'chach* lies flat without protruding downwards, and it is praiseworthy to chop off these branches or weave them into the existing *s'chach*.

Chapter Five

Sitting in the Succah

64. Why are we commanded to sit in a succah?

The Torah says "You shall dwell in booths for seven days, every citizen of Israel shall dwell in booths. In order that your generations shall know that I caused the children of Israel to dwell in booths when I brought them out from the land of Egypt" (*Vayikra* 23, 42-43). When the Jewish people left Egypt and traveled into the wilderness they numbered about three million people. The wilderness was a place of great desolation inhabited by deadly snakes and serpents, and there was no protection from the burning heat of the sun. Hashem therefore miraculously protected His chosen nation by surrounding them with seven clouds of glory - four around the sides, one above them, one below them like a carpet and one to lead the way. We are commanded to sit in a succah to remember this wonderful and miraculous act of kindness.

65. Why is this mitzvah performed in the month of Tishrei?

Although the Jewish people left Egypt in the month of Nissan and experienced the protection of Hashem's clouds of glory immediately, nevertheless the mitzvah of succah was postponed until Tishrei. Among the many reasons given are:

- Nissan marks the beginning of spring when the weather becomes warmer, and people naturally leave their houses to sit outdoors. Tishrei marks the beginning of fall when the weather becomes colder and people naturally return to the shelter of their homes and no longer sit outdoors. It is Hashem's wish that we sit in a succah in Tishrei to demonstrate that we do so solely to fulfill his commandment and not for our own convenience.

- The clouds of glory, which initially accompanied the Jewish people in the month of Nissan, were later removed when the golden calf was made. They returned permanently in the month of Tishrei when the construction of the tabernacle began, remaining with them for the entire forty years in the wilderness.

- On Rosh Hashanah and Yom Kippur, Hashem sits in judgement and decrees the fate of all mankind. In case some people were sentenced to be exiled from their homes, we build a succah and leave our houses.

66. How much time should one spend in the succah?

The Sages say, "For the entire seven days, a person should consider the succah to be his permanent home and his house to be a temporary place". Therefore, a person should eat, sleep and spend his time in the succah in the same way that he does in the house during the year. He fulfills a Torah commandment every single moment that he spends in the succah, both day and night.

67. Is it forbidden to leave the succah unnecessarily?

A person should live in the succah in the same manner that he lives at home during the year. Just as he naturally leaves his home to do certain activities and attend to various needs, so too may he leave the succah when the occasion demands it. Nevertheless, it is praiseworthy to maximize the amount of time spent in the succah since every moment brings eternal reward. If a person would be promised a vast sum of money for remaining in his house, would he not stay there as long as possible? Certainly he should stay in the succah where the reward is immeasurable! In certain circumstances, a person should leave the succah - see chapters ten and eleven.

68. When is one obligated to be in the succah?

There are three occasions:
• On the first night of Succos (see chapter eight).
• When eating a meal (see chapter six).
• When sleeping (see chapter seven).

69. Are women obligated to sit in the succah?

No. Women are exempt from this mitzvah since it is a positive mitzvah bound by time.

70. Should women make an effort to sit in the succah?

A woman who sits in the succah fulfills a Torah mitzvah. She should make an effort to do so for two reasons:

- The Divine Presence rests upon the succah. Every person who sits in the succah experiences a spiritual elevation and a cleansing of the soul.

- When a married woman sits in the succah with her husband, she enhances his mitzvah, since this is the way he lives in the house during the year.

71. Do women recite the *b'racha* for the succah?

See question 130.

72. Where should a woman kindle the Shabbos and Yom Tov lights?

She should kindle them in the succah, since the main mitzvah is to enjoy the lights during the meal. However, if there is a concern that they may be extinguished by the wind, or they may ח"ו be a fire risk, she should kindle them in the house. In this case, they should be placed near a window that faces the succah, if this is possible.

73. Are children obligated in the mitzvah of succah?

Boys from the age of five or six should be trained to fulfill the mitzvah (compare question 399).

74. Are boys obligated to sleep in the succah?

Yes. However, if they are afraid to sleep there or if it is too cold for them, they are exempt (see also question 179).

75. Is it better to learn Torah in the succah or in shul?

If a person is able to concentrate properly while in the succah he should learn Torah there. However, if this is difficult due to extreme weather conditions, disturbing noises etc, he should learn in shul or in the house. Similarly, if he requires many *sefarim* and it is troublesome to bring them all into the succah, he is not required to learn there. Nevertheless, if he is able to find sufficient space in the succah to store his *sefarim*, he is obligated to do so.

76. Is it better to *daven* in the succah or in shul?

• A man is obligated to *daven* with a *minyan* in shul. Just as he leaves his house to go to shul, he should also leave the succah to go to shul.

• If a man does not have a *minyan* in a shul which he can join, he may *daven* wherever he is able to concentrate - in shul, in the succah, or in the house. A woman should *daven* where she can concentrate best.

77.   Is it better to discuss business matters outside the succah?

Ideally, one should minimize mundane talk while in the succah (see question 193). Nevertheless, if a person needs to discuss business matters with a friend, he may do so and should not leave the succah.

Chapter Six

Eating in the Succah

78. Is a man obligated to eat everything inside the succah?

Strictly speaking, only meals must be eaten in the succah, but not snacks or drinks. However, it is praiseworthy to eat and drink everything inside the succah.

79. What constitutes a meal?

- A piece of bread larger than a *kebeitza*.
- According to some opinions, a piece of bread the size of a *kezayis* when accompanied by other foods constitutes a meal. Since this is disputed, a person should preferably eat such a meal in the succah, but he should not recite the *b'racha* for the succah (see question 113). Alternatively, he should eat more bread and recite the *b'racha* for the succah.

80. What if a person eats an entire meal without bread?

Strictly speaking, he is not required to eat in the succah, but he is strongly recommended to do so. The *b'racha* for the succah should not be recited unless the meal includes *mezonos* (see questions 114 and 115).

81. Must one eat *mezonos* foods in the succah?

There are different opinions about this, but the prevalent custom is to be strict and equate *mezonos* foods with bread. Therefore, one should not eat outside the succah a piece of *mezonos* food larger than a *kebeitza*. Regarding the *b'racha* for the succah, see question 114. In this context, rice is not regarded as a *mezonos* food.

82. May one eat or drink outside the succah during a meal?

If a person is eating a meal in the succah, everything he eats is considered to be part of the meal. Therefore, he is forbidden to have any food or drink outside the succah. He must be particularly careful to remember this when going to and from the house during the meal.

83. Must there be a table in the succah when eating?

If a person eats at a table that is not inside the succah, he does not fulfill the mitzvah. The reason is that we are concerned maybe he will be drawn towards the table and inadvertently eat outside the succah. One should be particularly careful when the table is in an invalid part of the succah. Therefore,

• If a person does not require a table he does not need to bring one into the succah.

• If he wishes to eat at a table, it must be brought inside the succah.

84.   What if part of the table is inside and part outside the succah?

This is permitted if at least 8cm of the table are inside the succah. It is preferable though to ensure that most of the table is inside the succah.

Chapter Seven
Sleeping in the Succah

85.   Is one obligated to sleep in the succah?

During the week of Succos, the succah is to be considered as a person's home. Since the primary activities of the home are eating and sleeping, a man is obligated to sleep in the succah. According to some opinions, sleeping in the succah is even more important than eating there.

86.   Why are many people lenient and sleep in the house?

There are two main reasons:
- In many countries, the weather is cold at this time of year, and sleeping in the succah would cause much discomfort (see questions 167-169).
- Women do not usually sleep in the succah, and if a married man would sleep in the succah leaving his wife alone in the house, this may cause him distress.

87.   May one rely on these leniences?

- Cold weather is certainly a valid reason. Indeed, if a person insists on sleeping in the succah when it is uncomfortably cold, he is considered to be foolish. However, it is praiseworthy to organize a way to heat the succah at night in order to be able to perform this important mitzvah. In countries such as *Eretz Yisrael* that usually have mild weather at Succos, the men should certainly sleep in the succah.

- The second reason obviously does not apply to single men nor to married men during the day. Similarly, if a wife does not mind her husband sleeping in the succah at night, he should do so.

Whoever is meticulous to sleep in the succah and fulfill the mitzvah properly will merit seeing the Divine Presence.

88.   May one sleep alone in the succah?

Although a person should avoid sleeping alone in a house, he is permitted to sleep alone in the succah, since he is performing a mitzvah. In addition, the Divine Presence rests upon the succah and protects a person from all dangers.

89.   What if a person is nevertheless afraid to sleep in the succah?

Then he is permitted to sleep in the house. If a person lives in a dangerous area and sleeping in the succah is an obvious danger, he should act sensibly and not rely upon miracles.

90.   May one build a succah in a place where he is afraid to sleep?

According to most opinions, a succah that is suitable only for eating but not for sleeping is *possul*. Since a succah is intended to be a person's home, it must be suitable for both eating and sleeping. Therefore, every effort should be made to build the succah in a location that is safe enough for sleeping. In extenuating circumstances, a rav should be consulted. (See question 172.)

91.   What if there is not enough room in the succah for all the men of the family to sleep?

- If there is only room for one, the father should sleep there.
- If there is also room for one son, the sons should take turns on different nights.
- Boys above bar mitzvah take precedence over those below bar mitzvah.

92.   May one sleep in the succah with his legs outside the succah (or in an invalid section of the succah)?

If his head and most of his body are inside the succah, he fulfills the mitzvah, and he is obligated to sleep in the succah in that manner.

93.   What if he is forced to sleep in a cramped position in a small area?

He is required to do so. However, a person is exempt from sleeping in such a position if

- the succah was originally spacious but later became cramped **and** he is a finicky person who would be disturbed **or**
- he is an extremely finicky person who would be greatly disturbed.

94.   Must there be a table in the succah when sleeping?

No, this is unnecessary (compare question 83).

95.   If the table is left in the succah, may one sleep underneath it?

Ideally, one should eat and sleep in the succah with nothing intervening between him and the *s'chach*. However, if necessary, it is permitted to sleep under a standard table (since it is less than 80cm high).

96.   May one sleep in the lower bed of a bunk bed?

This is permitted if the space between the beds is less than 80cm. This is true even if the upper bed is more than this distance from the ground, and even if someone is sleeping in the upper bed.

97.   May one take a short nap outside the succah?

No, this is forbidden. Although a person may eat a snack outside the succah (see question 78), he may not sleep even for a few moments outside the succah. The reason is that sometimes even a short nap is satisfying and beneficial to a person and is equivalent to a proper sleep.

98.   Must one avoid dozing outside the succah?

• If a person is in his house (in an armchair etc.) he must avoid dozing.

- If he is not home (e.g. travelling, in shul etc.) he is not required to avoid dozing since in this situation he is exempt from the mitzvah of succah. Nevertheless, it is praiseworthy to avoid dozing, since according to some opinions it is forbidden to do so outside the succah even in these situations.

99. Should one awaken a person who has accidentally fallen asleep outside the succah?

No. Although initially it may have been forbidden for him to doze outside the succah, nevertheless he is now exempt since it is a distress to be awakened and moved.

100. What if one cannot sleep in the succah due to noise etc?

In this situation, he is exempt from the mitzvah and may sleep in the house (see chapter eleven).

Chapter Eight

The First Night of Succos

101. How is the first night different from the rest of Succos?

By a comparison of verses, we deduce that the mitzvah of eating in the succah on the first night of Succos is parallel to the mitzvah of eating matzo on the first night of Pesach. Therefore, on the first night of Succos, men are obligated by the Torah to eat in the succah. During the rest of Succos, they are obligated to eat in the succah only if they want to have a meal (see question 78).

102. How much must a man eat?

Preferably, he should eat a piece of bread the size of a *kebeitza*, but if this is difficult he may eat a piece the size of a *kezayis*. Since this is a Torah obligation, one should preferably use the stricter measurements (see appendix).

103. Is this also an obligation on the second night in *chutz la'aretz*?

Yes. However, since this is a Rabbinic obligation, one may use the lenient measurements (compare previous question).

104. May one eat the *kezayis* before nightfall?

No. The first *kezayis* of bread must be eaten after nightfall. If a person mistakenly began the meal before nightfall he must eat another *kezayis* of bread after nightfall, but should not repeat the *b'racha* for the succah.

105. How quickly should the bread be eaten?

A *kezayis* of bread must be eaten within two minutes if possible, or at least four minutes. Special care should be taken not to speak until the *kezayis* has been eaten.

106. May the bread be eaten with honey or other accompaniments?

According to most opinions this is permitted. Some opinions require that one eat this quantity without any accompaniment, parallel to the *kezayis* matzo eaten on the first night of Pesach.

107. What should a person think when eating the first *kezayis*?

He should think about the following two ideas:

- He is fulfilling the Torah mitzvah to sit in the succah.
- The succah is a reminder of the exodus from Egypt, and the clouds of glory that surrounded the Jewish people in the wilderness protecting them from all harm (see question 64).

108. What if he did not think about this?

•   If he thought that he is fulfilling the mitzvah of succah, he has fulfilled his obligation, although he did not think about the reasons. Nevertheless, it is preferable to eat another *kezayis* with the complete intention, since according to some opinions, he has not fulfilled his obligation.

•   If he did not even think about fulfilling the mitzvah, he has not fulfilled his obligation, and he is required to eat another *kezayis* with the correct intention.

109. Must one think about this every time he enters the succah during Succos?

It is preferable to do so, since according to some opinions, one does not fulfill the mitzvah otherwise.

110. Is eating restricted on *erev* Succos?

The first *kezayis* of bread should be eaten in the succah with appetite, parallel to the first *kezayis* of matzo on Pesach. Therefore, men may not eat bread or *mezonos* foods (except rice) from the beginning of the tenth *halachic* hour of the day (i.e halfway between *halachic* midday and sunset).

111. What if it is raining on the first night?

See question 157.

Chapter Nine

The B'racha for the Succah

112. Which *b'racha* is recited for the succah?

אשר קדשנו במצותיו וצונו לישב בסוכה.

113. Is the *b'racha* always recited when eating in the succah?

No. It is usually recited only when eating a piece of bread larger than a *kebeitza*. On the first night, it is recited when eating a *kezayis* of bread (see question 102).

114. Is the *b'racha* recited when eating *mezonos* foods (except rice)?

- If he is eating it as a meal, he should recite the *b'racha*.

- If he is eating it as a snack, opinions differ about this. The main custom is to recite the *b'racha* for a baked *mezonos* food (e.g. cake, crackers) that is larger than a *kebeitza*. In such a case, it is preferable to remain a while in the succah and not leave immediately after eating, so that the *b'racha* can also apply to the continued sitting in the succah.

- If he is eating it at *kiddush* on Shabbos or Yom Tov, he should recite the *b'racha*.

115. Is the *b'racha* recited over other foods?

No. Even if one ate an entire meal he does not recite the *b'racha* unless he eats bread or *mezonos*. Nevertheless, it is praiseworthy to ask someone who is reciting the *b'racha* to include him with the *b'racha*.

116. Is the *b'racha* recited when sleeping or when just sitting in the succah?

According to the widely accepted custom, the *b'racha* is recited only when eating bread or *mezonos*. Some have the custom to recite the *b'racha* every time they enter the succah (after a significant break) even if they do not intend to eat bread or *mezonos*. Ideally, a person should eat some *mezonos* in order to recite the *b'racha*.

117. What is the reason for the first custom?

Although a person fulfills a Torah mitzvah every moment that he is inside the succah, the *b'racha* was ordained to be recited only when doing a significant action. Eating was chosen as the most significant activity, and all other activities such as sitting and sleeping are included in the *b'racha* that is recited when eating.

118. What if he does not intend eating immediately?

Ideally, he should eat some *mezonos* immediately in order to recite the *b'racha* for the succah as soon as possible. If he does not wish to do so, he should postpone reciting the *b'racha* for the succah until he is ready to eat. The *b'racha* will then apply retroactively to the entire time that he has been sitting in the succah.

119. Is the *b'racha* for the succah recited before the *b'racha* for the food?

- When eating bread, the *b'racha hamotzi* is recited before the *b'racha* for the succah.
- When eating *mezonos*, the main custom is to recite the *b'racha mezonos* first, but some have the custom to recite the *b'racha* for the succah first.

120. When is the *b'racha* recited when reciting *kiddush*?

- When *kiddush* is recited in the evening of Shabbos or Yom Tov, the *b'racha* for the succah is included in the *kiddush*.
- When *kiddush* is recited in the morning and is followed by *mezonos*, the *b'racha* for the succah is included in the *kiddush*.
- When *kiddush* is recited in the morning and is followed by bread, there are two customs. Some include the *b'racha* for the succah in the *kiddush* and some recite the *b'racha* together with the *b'racha hamotzi*. Both customs are equally acceptable.

121. Is the *b'racha* recited when making *havdalah*?

Although *havdalah* should be recited in the succah, there are different customs regarding the *b'racha* for the succah:

- Some include the *b'racha* at the end of *havdalah*.
- Some recite the *b'racha* at the start of *havdalah*.
- Some do not recite the *b'racha* at all.

The most ideal procedure would be to eat some bread or *mezonos* after *havdalah* and recite the *b'racha* for the succah with the *b'racha* for the food.

122. What if a person forgot to say the *b'racha* and began a meal?

He should recite the *b'racha* as soon as he remembers and eat some more.

123. What if he already bensched?

He should say the *b'racha* if he still intends to remain a while in the succah.

124. Does the *b'racha* last all day?

• If a person remains in the succah all day or leaves for a short break, he does not repeat the *b'racha*. This is true even if he eats another meal.

• If he leaves for a significant break, he should repeat the *b'racha* the next time he eats bread or *mezonos*.

125. What is considered a significant break?

• To *daven shacharis*.
• To *daven mincha* **and** *ma'ariv*.
• To leave for two hours.
• To leave due to heavy rain (see question 151).

126. What if he leaves to *daven mincha* or *ma'ariv*?

There are different opinions about this. A suggested compromise is to repeat the *b'racha* the next time that he eats bread, but not if he eats only *mezonos*.

127. What if he leaves to *daven mincha* or *ma'ariv* in the middle of a meal?

A new *b'racha* should not be made.

128. What if he intended to leave for two hours but in fact returned sooner?

Since he took his mind off the succah, he must make a new *b'racha* when eating bread or *mezonos*. This is true even if he changed his mind and returned immediately.

129. If a person goes to a different succah, does he recite a new *b'racha*?

The above rules are the same whether he returns to the original succah or goes to another succah. This is true even if the second succah belongs to someone else, and even if he did not have the second succah in mind when he made the original *b'racha*. This is because the mitzvah is the same in whichever succah one sits, and walking to another succah is not considered to be an interruption. However, since some opinions disagree with this analysis, it is preferable to have the second succah in mind when making the original *b'racha*.

130. Do women recite the *b'racha*?

According to the *Ashkenazic* custom, women recite the *b'racha* in the same situations that men do.

131. Should the *b'racha* be recited when standing or sitting?

According to the *Ashkenazic* custom, the *b'racha* is recited when sitting. If *kiddush* is recited standing, some have the custom to remain standing until after the *b'racha* for the succah, and some sit down before the *b'racha* for the succah.

132. Is the *b'racha shehecheyanu* recited for the succah?

Yes, it is recited the first time one eats in the succah. This is usually on the first night of Succos, in which case the *b'racha* is included in *kiddush*.

133. What is the order of *brachos* in *kiddush* on the first night?

1. ‫בורא פרי הגפן‬.
2. ‫אשר בחר בנו‬.
3. ‫לישב בסוכה‬.
4. ‫שהחיינו‬.

134. Why is *shehecheyanu* recited last?

Because it serves a dual purpose:
- For the new Yom Tov and
- For the new *mitzvah* of sitting in the succah.

One should think about this when saying or listening to the *b'racha*.

135. What if he said *shehecheyanu* before לישב בסוכה?

He does not repeat anything.

136. What if he ate in the house on the first night (e.g. it was raining)?

Although he does recite *shehecheyanu* during *kiddush* in the house for the Yom Tov, he must repeat *shehecheyanu* for the succah when he eats the first meal there.

137. What is the order of *brachos* in *kiddush* on the second night in *chutz la'aretz*?

The main custom is to reverse the order of the last two *brachos*, i.e. to say *shehecheyanu* before לישב בסוכה, unless this is the first time he is eating in the succah. Some have the custom not to reverse the order in any event.

138. What if the second night is *motzai* Shabbos (in *chutz la'aretz*)?

Then six brachos are recited in the following order:

1. בורא פרי הגפן.
2. אשר בחר בנו.
3. בורא מאורי האש.
4. המבדיל.
5. שהחיינו.
6. לישב בסוכה.

(Some reverse the order of the last two *brachos*.)

139. What if a person made *kiddush* and then realized that the succah roof was closed?

He does not need to repeat any of the *kiddush* except for the *b'racha* on the succah which must be repeated after opening the roof (compare question 153).

Chapter Ten

Rain

140. Is a person obligated to eat in the succah when it is raining?

- If it is raining heavily, he is not obligated to eat there (except on the first night - see question 157).
- If it is raining lightly, he is obligated to eat there.

141. What is considered heavy rain?

When the rain is coming through the *s'chach* into the succah to the extent that if this would be happening in his house he would leave the room.

142. What if he is uncertain if he would leave the room in his house?

He should remain in the succah until he no longer has any doubt.

143. What if he cannot feel the rain where he is sitting?

Then he is obligated to eat in the succah, but it is questionable whether he may recite the *b'racha* for the succah.

144. What if he is a sensitive person who is disturbed by even light rain?

He is permitted to leave the succah even though most people would not.

145. What if it begins to rain when sleeping in the succah?

Since even a few drops of rain cause distress when sleeping, he is permitted to leave the succah immediately.

146. What if the sky is overcast and it is certain to rain soon?

One is still obligated to eat and sleep in the succah until it actually begins to rain.

147. Is one permitted to remain in the succah when it rains?

If it is raining to the degree that he is exempt from the mitzvah then he should leave. A person who thinks that he is fulfilling a mitzvah by going beyond the line of duty in this situation is regarded as foolish and receives no reward. It is certainly forbidden to recite the *b'racha* for the succah (see question 171).

148. What should the attitude be when leaving the succah due to rain?

One should feel humble and upset at the fact that he has been prevented from performing a mitzvah. Such a situation is compared to a servant who brought a drink to his master, whereupon the master took the drink and threw it in the face of the servant. (This applies only in *Eretz Yisrael* if the rain arrives unexpectedly.)

149. Is one obligated to return to the succah as soon as the rain stops?

- If he did not yet sit down to eat in the house he must go to eat in the succah, even if he left the succah in the middle of a meal.
- If he is in the middle of eating in the house, he may remain there until the end of the meal.
- If he went to sleep at night in the house due to rain he may remain in the house until the morning.

In the last two cases, it is praiseworthy to return to the succah immediately, although he is not obligated to do so.

150. Does the same apply to a succah with a roof that is easy to open and close?

If a person closes the roof and remains in the succah while it is raining, he is obligated to open the roof again as soon as he realizes that it has stopped raining. This is true even if he is in the middle of eating or sleeping.

151. When a person returns to the succah after the rain stops, does he repeat the *b'racha* for the succah?

Since it is impossible to fulfill the mitzvah while it is raining, the previous *b'racha* is no longer valid. Therefore, he should repeat the *b'racha* when he next eats bread or *mezonos*.

152. What if it has stopped raining but it is still dripping into the succah?

If it is not difficult to go to someone else's succah he is obligated to do so. If this is difficult, he may remain in the house.

153. What if a person began eating in the succah and recited the *b'racha* for the succah and then realized that the roof was closed?

He must open the roof and repeat the *b'racha* for the succah (see also question 139).

154. May one open and close the roof on Shabbos and Yom Tov?

Yes, since this is like opening and closing a door. However, when opening the roof after rain, care must be taken not to cause water to spill directly onto grass or plants.

155. What can be done to avoid the water spilling onto grass?

It is permitted to open the roof if the water will spill onto the grass indirectly. Therefore, if the water falls onto a paved area and from there rolls onto the grass, this is permitted. If the grass is adjacent to the succah, one should place boards or plastic sheets over the grass (before Shabbos or Yom Tov) to prevent the water from spilling directly onto the grass.

156. Does the same apply after a heavy rainfall?

After heavy rain when the grass has been thoroughly watered, it is very unlikely that a small amount of water from the succah roof will be of any benefit to the grass. Therefore, it is permitted to open the roof even if the water spills directly onto the grass.

157. What if it rains on the first night of Succos?

Opinions differ whether one is obligated to eat in the succah despite the rain. On one hand, there is a parallel to the first night of Pesach when one is obligated to eat matzo in any event, but on the other hand there is usually no mitzvah to sit in the succah when it rains. Therefore, one should wait an hour or two in the hope that the rain will stop in order to eat in the succah and fulfill the mitzvah properly. If after waiting it is still raining, see question 159.

158. What if the family cannot wait so long?

Then he is not required to wait and he should follow the procedure explained in question 159. The same applies if he has invited guests who are hungry and wish to eat immediately.

159. What is the procedure when it is still raining?

One should do the following:
1. Make *kiddush* in the succah omitting the *b'racha* for the succah.

2. Wash one's hands.
3. Say *hamotzi* and eat a *kezayis* of bread in the succah.
4. Eat the remainder of the meal in the house.
5. Bensch in the house.

160. Are women required to do the same?

Since women are exempt from the mitzvah of succah they are permitted to eat the entire meal in the house. However, they must also fulfill the mitzvah of *kiddush* in the .house and not in the succah. Therefore, if the succah is adjacent to the house, the women should listen to *kiddush* from the house. If they listen to *kiddush* in a room near the succah and wish to eat in another room they must eat at least one *kezayis* of bread in the first room. If from the second room they can see the place where they heard *kiddush*, they may eat their meal there. They should remember to recite the *shehecheyanu b'racha* for the succah when they eat the first meal there, unless they recited it when lighting candles there (see question 72).

161. What if the succah is far from the house?

If the women will not be able to hear *kiddush* from the house there are several options:
- They should do the same as the men (i.e. listen to *kiddush* and eat a *kezayis* of bread in the succah).
- One woman should recite *kiddush* for the women in the house.

- One man should recite *kiddush* for the women in the house before or after he has made or heard *kiddush* in the succah.

The first two alternatives are better than the third.

162. What if the rain stops during the meal?

The men should return to the succah, recite the *b'racha* for the succah and eat another piece of bread larger than a *kebeitza*. They should bensch in the succah. The women may do the same if they wish.

163. What if the rain stops only after bensching?

The men are required to fulfill the mitzvah of succah. They should wash again, recite *hamotzi* and the *b'racha* for the succah and eat a piece of bread larger than a *kebeitza*.

164. If the rain still continues how long should a man wait?

He should wait as long as he is able to, but if he feels very tired he may go to sleep for the night. If he exerts himself to remain awake until the rain stops and is able to fulfill the mitzvah, he is indeed praiseworthy.

165. What if it rains on the second night in *chutz la'aretz*?

He should wait a little while in the house in the hope that the rain will stop. If the rain continues he should make *kiddush* and begin the meal in the house. At the end of the meal he should go to the succah, eat a *kezayis* of bread and bensch there. The *b'racha* for the succah should not be recited. If the rain stops during or after the meal, see questions 162, 163.

Chapter Eleven

Special Exemptions

166. In which situations is a man exempt from the mitzvah of succah?

There are several types of situations in which a person is exempt:

- Discomfort.
- Sickness.
- Preoccupation with other mitzvos.
- Travel.

167. What is meant by discomfort?

This means that the conditions in the succah are causing him discomfort and he will gain relief by leaving the succah. If in the same circumstances he would leave the house, he is then permitted to leave the succah.

168. What are common examples?

A person is exempt in the following situations:

- The succah is too hot or too cold. If one can easily dress more warmly or heat the succah, he should do so (see question 87).
- There is an unpleasant smell.
- There are many insects in the succah.
- There is noise that is causing much disturbance.
- Leaves or twigs are falling into the food and he is very disturbed by this.

169. What if he feels discomfort when sleeping but not when eating?

Then he is exempted only from sleeping in the succah, but is obligated to eat there.

170. What if the lights accidentally go out on Friday night?

Since there is discomfort when eating in the dark, he is permitted to go into the house where there is light. However, if it is not difficult to go to someone else's succah, he is obligated to do so. On Yom Tov, it is permitted to light candles from an existing flame to illuminate the succah. One should take care that they do not blow out while carrying them.

171. Is there a mitzvah to remain in a succah despite the discomfort?

No. If he is exempt due to discomfort there is no mitzvah or reward in remaining there (see question 147). It is praiseworthy to try and make the succah comfortable in order to be able to remain there (see question 87).

172. What if the discomfort was inevitable due to the position of the succah?

It is forbidden to build a succah in such a position, and one cannot fulfill any mitzvah in such a succah. Care must be taken to choose a suitable site for the succah where one will be able to fulfill the mitzvah in normal circumstances. One may claim exemption only if the discomfort arose unexpectedly. In extenuating circumstances, a rav should be consulted. (See question 90.)

173. What if there is discomfort because the succah is small and cramped?

This is no excuse and he is obligated to eat and sleep in the succah. Obviously, one should have foresight to build a succah that will be large enough to accommodate the family comfortably (see also question 93).

174. What if a person feels distressed due to bad news?

He is obligated to be in the succah. This form of discomfort is not due to the succah and will not be alleviated by moving into the house.

175. Does discomfort exempt a person on the first night of Succos?

No. He is obligated to make *kiddush* and eat at least a *kezayis* of bread in the succah before moving into the house, but he should not recite the *b'racha* for the succah (see question 159).

176. Who is exempt due to sickness?

- A person who needs to be in bed.
- A person who has a pain and will feel more comfortable in the house than in the succah, e.g. headache, pain in the eyes etc.

177. Is a doctor exempt?

- A doctor who is on duty attending the sick is exempt.
- If he is presently off duty but is likely to be called upon at any time, he is also exempt unless being in the succah will not cause a delay when required.
- If he is off duty and not likely to be called at any time, he is obligated to eat and sleep in the succah.
- If he is taking care of a dangerously ill person, he is exempt even while he is not required.

178. What about a man who may need to attend to his young children at night?

If the succah is near to the house and he will be able to hear his children, he should sleep in the succah. Otherwise he is exempt and may sleep in the house.

179. What if a person has a tendency to catch a cold due to sleeping in the succah?

He is permitted to sleep in the house. This is particularly important for children, who are more prone to catch a cold.

180. Do the above laws for the sick, doctors etc. apply on the first night?

No, the law is the same as for exemption due to discomfort (see question 175). However, if there is a risk that the patient will become more ill because of the succah, he is exempt even on the first night.

181. When does preoccupation with mitzvos grant exemption?

If a person begins to perform a mitzvah and is thereby prevented from eating or sleeping in a succah, he is exempt. For example:

- He is on the way to visit his rav or parents.
- He is patrolling the streets to guard the town.

182. If he can find a succah is he obligated to do so?

If this does not involve much trouble he is obligated to find a succah for eating and sleeping (the town guard is exempt).

183. May a person visit his parents if they have no succah?

This is permitted even though he will not be able to eat or sleep in a succah. If he can make arrangements to eat and sleep at a neighbor's succah he should do so, unless this will upset his parents. A rav should be consulted for advice.

184. Should a bris be held in the succah?

The actual bris should not be held in the succah, since sanitary conditions cannot be guaranteed. The festive meal should be eaten in the succah.

185. What if the succah is too small for all the guests?

Then one should invite only as many men as the succah can accommodate (ten men are sufficient). The women may eat outside the succah.

186. At the bris (that is held indoors), who should drink the wine?

The man who recites the *b'racha* should drink less than a cheekful, since he is not in a succah.

187. What other festive meals must be held in a succah?

An engagement, *pidyon haben*, bar mitzvah, and *siyum* must all be held in a succah.

188. When is a traveler exempt?

If a person needs to travel (e.g. for business, to perform a mitzvah) during Succos he may do so, even though he will not be able to find a succah on the way. Just as a person leaves his house in order to travel, so too may he leave the succah in order to travel. Therefore, he may eat freely while traveling, unless he can easily find a succah along the way.

189. What about sleeping overnight?

He must make an effort to find a succah to sleep in, but if he is unsuccessful he may sleep indoors.

190. What about pleasure trips?

It is forbidden to eat or sleep outside a succah if one is travelling only for pleasure. People who go on trips to places where there is no succah and then claim exemption are transgressing.

Chapter Twelve

Honoring the Succah

191. Does the succah have special sanctity?

Yes, the succah has great sanctity. According to the *Zohar*, the Divine Presence rests upon the succah, and the souls of seven of our great ancestors visit every day (see question 221). Furthermore, the word succah hints at the two primary names of Hashem – the four lettered name beginning with *'yud'* has the same numerical value of the central two letters (ו"כ=26), and the four lettered name beginning with *'aleph'* has the same numerical value as the outer two letters (ה"ס=65).

192. Which laws apply to this sanctity?

There are two issues involved:
- Behavior inside the succah must be dignified.
- Personal use of the succah is limited.

193. What is meant by dignified behavior?

A person should minimize mundane talk in the succah, and try to speak only words of Torah and holy matters. Certainly, one must be extremely careful not to speak *lashon harah* or become angry while in the succah (see question 77).

194. What are the restrictions on personal use?

It is forbidden to remove any part of the walls or *s'chach* for personal use, since this degrades its sanctity. All normal use of the succah is permitted, since one is expected to live in a succah in the same way that one lives in a house. For example, one may hang items or lean on the walls and take shelter from the sun by standing in or near the succah.

195. Do the decorations also have sanctity?

Yes, all the decorations whether hanging from the *s'chach* or on the walls have such sanctity. Therefore, they may not be removed from the succah for personal use. For example, fruit which is hung from the *s'chach* may not be removed and eaten until after Succos. Pictures that are hung on the walls may not be removed and re-hung in the house until after Succos.

196. May one remove decorations because of the rain?

Decorations may be removed on *chol hamoed* and brought into the house to prevent them from being spoiled by the rain. They may be returned later to the succah, but may not be used in the house until after Succos.

197. What if decorations fall down by themselves?

The same restrictions apply. However, they may be re-hung in the succah on *chol hamoed*.

198. What if *s'chach* or decorations fall down on Shabbos or Yom Tov?

They are *muktzeh* and may not be moved directly with one's hands. If they fall onto the table, one may push them off with one's elbow.

199. Are they *muktzeh* while still hanging in the succah?

Yes. On Shabbos and Yom Tov, the *s'chach* and decorations are *muktzeh* even while still in place. Therefore, care must be taken not to move drapes, paper chains etc. with one's hands while inside the succah.

200. Can one prevent the decorations from becoming sanctified?

Yes. If a condition is made before Yom Tov, the decorations attached to the walls do not become sanctified. This will allow a person to make personal use of them, and will prevent them from becoming *muktzeh* on Shabbos and Yom Tov. This condition does not affect the decorations that are attached to the *s'chach* and they remain sanctified nevertheless.

201. What is the condition that must be made?

One should say "I do not withhold use of the decorations during the entire period of *bein hashmashos* (i.e. from sunset until nightfall) for all the seven days of Succos". In *chutz la'aretz*, one should conclude "for all the eight days of Succos".

202. When should this be said?

Any time after the decorations are placed in the succah until sunset on the first evening of Succos.

203. Must the condition be verbalized or is it sufficient to think it?

The condition must be verbalized.

204. May decorations be removed on Shabbos and Yom Tov if the condition was made?

Although the condition prevents the decorations from becoming *muktzeh*, this does not automatically permit one to remove them from the succah on Shabbos or Yom Tov. If the decorations are tied or pinned to the walls, it is forbidden to remove them on Shabbos or Yom Tov due to the prohibition of demolishing. They may be removed only if they are hanging on a hook or tied to the succah with a bow.

205. Does the succah have any sanctity after Succos?

After Succos, the succah loses its sanctity and one may use the walls and the *s'chach* for any other purpose. Nevertheless, one must not disgrace them by treading on them or throwing them in the street. It is certainly forbidden to throw them into the garbage. If one wishes to discard them without disgracing them, one may burn them. (See also questions 421 and 422)

206. May one throw away used decorations?

Used decorations may be thrown away if they are properly wrapped up in a bag. If they contain verses or other words of Torah they must be buried with *sheimos* (see question 60).

207. How should one honor the succah?

By decorating the succah beautifully and by avoiding disrespectful activities.

208. Which activities are disrespectful?

The following are common examples:
- Bringing pots and pans inside.
- Leaving dirty plates inside.
- Washing dishes.
- Using the succah as a storeroom.

209. Is it actually forbidden to bring pots and pans inside?

Strictly speaking it is permitted, but the accepted custom is to avoid it. Therefore, one should transfer the food to plates or serving dishes outside the succah.

210. If a pot was brought inside, is the succah still kosher?

Opinions differ about this. Therefore, one should not recite the *b'racha* for the succah if a pot is inside.

211. How quickly must the dirty plates be removed?

According to some opinions, they should be removed immediately after the food has been eaten. However, the custom is to be lenient and leave the plates in the succah until it is convenient to remove them. This is because the succah should be treated like one's home, and dirty plates are not always removed immediately from the table.

212. May dirty plates be removed close to nightfall on Shabbos?

During the year, it is forbidden to clear the table after the third meal close to the end of Shabbos since it is considered to be preparing for *motzai* Shabbos. However, on Succos one should do so since one is thereby honoring the succah immediately.

213. May one put pots and dirty plates in a section of the succah that is invalid?

Yes, but according to some opinions, this should be avoided.

214. Is it forbidden to wash all types of dishes in the succah?

It is permitted to rinse cups in the succah, but not other dishes or cutlery.

215. What is meant by using the succah as a storeroom?

Any item that one would not leave in his dining room should not be left in the succah, e.g. bicycle, broom, etc.

216. May one have a garbage bin in the succah?

If he would put it in his dining room, he may put it in the succah.

217. May one wash *nagel-vasser* in the succah?

This is permitted, since it is correct to wash one's hands by the bedside. However, the used water should be removed as soon as possible.

218. May one wash hands for a meal inside the succah?

One may wash in the succah, but the used water should be removed as soon as possible. If one washes outside the succah, this may create a *halachic* problem on Shabbos and Yom Tov, since ideally one should not change location between *kiddush* and the meal. The custom is to be lenient about this is on Succos, but it would be correct to organize a way to wash hands inside or close to the succah. (Care must be taken to avoid spilling water onto grass and plants - see question 154).

219. May one hang wet laundry inside a succah?

No, this is forbidden.

220. May one invite a gentile into the succah?

This should be avoided if possible. According to some opinions, the succah loses its special sanctity when a gentile is present.

221. What is the meaning of *Ushpizin*?

Ushpizin means 'guests'. According to the *Zohar*, the souls of seven forefathers descend from *Gan Eden* and enter the succah as special guests. They are Avraham, Yitzchok, Ya'akov, Moshe, Aharon, Yossef and Dovid. All seven visit the succah every day, with a different one leading the others on each day. Some have the custom to invite the guests using a text found in the siddur or *machzor*. This is said at the start of every meal, both at night and at day, since the guests do not enter the succah unless they are verbally invited. It is also proper to invite human guests, i.e. poor people, to share in the meals in the succah, since this gives pleasure to the spiritual guests. If one cannot find poor people to invite, he should donate money to charity before Succos, to enable poor people to buy their Yom Tov meals. By doing this it will be regarded as if they were guests in his succah.

222. What is *simchas beis hashoevah*?

In the days of the Temple, the daily morning sacrifice was accompanied by a special water libation during the seven days of Succos. Each evening during *chol hamoed*, water was drawn from a pool on the outskirts of Jerusalem and brought to the Temple in preparation for the following day's offering. Throughout the entire night, a huge multitude of people watched pious men and elders sing and dance with lighted torches, to the accompaniment of music played by numerous Levites with harps, cymbals, trumpets and many other instruments. Our Sages comment, "Whoever did not see this rejoicing never saw rejoicing in his life". When Yonah participated in this festivity, the Holy Spirit rested on him and he attained the level of prophecy. The phrase *simchas beis hashoevah'* literally means the rejoicing at the place of water drawing, and is based on the verse (Isiah 12, 3) "And you shall draw water with joy from the wells of salvation". Today, many have the custom to dance and sing praises to Hashem in the evenings of *chol hamoed* in remembrance of the Temple festivities.

223. May a visitor from *chutz la'aretz* participate in a *simchas beis hashoevah* on the first night of *chol hamoed*?

Although for such a visitor it is the second day of Yom Tov, he may participate in a *simchas beis hashoevah*. He may listen to the music and join in the singing and dancing, since this is a mitzvah.

Chapter Thirteen

The Last Days of Succos

224. When should furniture be moved from the succah to the house?

On *Hoshanah Rabba* (or *Shemini Atzeres* in *chutz la'aretz*), one should move furniture back into the house in preparation for the evening. This may be done from *mincha ketana* (two-and-a-half *halachic* hours before sunset).

225. Is it permitted to do this any earlier?

No, since this is disrespectful to the succah, which is supposed to be one's home for the entire duration of Succos. After *mincha ketana* it is permitted, since it is then clear that one is doing it in honor of the approaching festival.

226. Is there anything special to do when finally parting with the succah?

Some have the custom to kiss the succah. Many have the custom to say a special prayer in which one expresses the wish to be worthy to sit in the succah reserved for the righteous in the world to come.

227. When is this done?

Close to sunset at the end of *Hoshanah Rabbah* (or *Shemini Atzeres* in *chutz la'aretz*).

228. Is there an obligation to sit in the succah on *Shemini Atzeres* in *chutz la'aretz*?

According to most opinions, the Yom Tov meals must be eaten in the succah. The *b'racha* for the succah is certainly not recited. One may have snacks and drinks in the house, since even on Succos there is no obligation to have them in the succah. Some have the custom to be lenient on *Shemini Atzeres* and eat some or all of the Yom Tov meal in the house. A person should not be lenient unless he has a strong family custom regarding this.

229. What about sleeping in the succah on *Shemini Atzeres* in *chutz la'aretz*?

The widespread custom is to be lenient about this and permit sleeping in the house. According to some opinions, one should sleep in the succah.

230. Should a visitor from *Eretz Yisrael* eat in the succah on *Shemini Atzeres* in *chutz la'aretz*?

According to some opinions, he is required to eat the Yom Tov meals in the succah, but he should think that he is not doing so in order to fulfill the mitzvah. He should also secretly try to eat part of the meal outside the succah. According to other opinions, he may eat inside the house if there are other residents of that town who have the custom to eat the meals inside the house.

231. Should a visitor from *chutz la'aretz* eat in the succah on *Shemini Atzeres* in *Eretz Yisrael*?

If a person has a custom not to eat in the succah when he is in *chutz la'aretz*, he is not required to do so when in *Eretz Yisrael*. If he does eat in the succah in *chutz la'aretz*, the following rules apply:

- According to some opinions, he is required to eat the Yom Tov meals in the succah, even if his host is eating in the house. Although this may involve some distress, he is not excused. Some opinions add that a cooking pot should be brought into the succah during the meal, in order to demonstrate that he is not openly deviating from the local custom.

- According to other opinions, he is not required to eat in the succah, since all the residents of *Eretz Yisrael* eat in the house.

232. May a resident of *Eretz Yisrael* eat or sleep in the succah on *Shemini Atzeres*?

If he wishes to do so, he must remove some of the *s'chach* before Yom Tov to demonstrate that he is not sitting there in order to fulfill a mitzvah. The area removed should be at least 32cm x 32cm.

233. May a resident of *chutz la'aretz* eat or sleep in the succah on *Simchas Torah*?

In this case too, he is required to do something to the succah to demonstrate that he is not sitting there in order to fulfill a mitzvah. However, since *Shemini Atzeres* is Yom Tov, he cannot remove a section of the *s'chach*, but rather he should bring a cooking pot into the succah.

234. May one eat or sleep in the succah on *Isru Chag*?

From *Isru chag* onwards, one may eat or sleep in the succah without making any alterations to it. Since Yom Tov is over, it does not appear as though he intends to fulfill a mitzvah.

Chapter Fourteen
The Four Species

235. What do the four species signify?

The *midrashic* literature is replete with explanations and allusions for the four species. The following is a selection:

- The esrog, which has taste and fragrance, represents Jews who possess both Torah and good deeds. The palm, whose fruit has taste but no fragrance, represents Jews who possess Torah but lack good deeds. The hadas, which has fragrance but no taste, represents Jews who possess good deeds but lack Torah. The aravah, which has neither taste nor fragrance, represents Jews who lack both Torah and good deeds. Hashem does not wish to destroy any of them, therefore he instructs us to bind them all together so that one will atone for the other.

- The esrog, which resembles a person's heart, atones for evil thoughts of the heart. The hadas, which resembles the eyes, atones for sinful sights. The aravah, which resembles the lips, atones for sinful speech. The lulav, which resembles the spine, represents Israel's upright devotion to Hashem. By taking the four species together a person declares his complete dedication to Hashem.

- This may be compared to two people who came before a judge for a dispute, and it is not known who was victorious. When one of them emerges with a scepter in his hand, it is a sign that he triumphed. Similarly, Israel and the other nations come in conflict before Hashem on Rosh Hashanah and we do not know who prevailed. But when Israel emerges with the lulav and esrog in their hands it is a sign that they are the victors.

236. Should the species be taken to a rav to be checked?

Yes. Even if they have a reliable *hechsher* indicating that they may be used to fulfill the mitzvah, they should be taken to a rav. Since huge quantities are checked and something may be overlooked, they should be inspected by an expert. Additionally, the species may deteriorate between the time of packaging and the purchase. Certainly, if a person is in doubt about the kashrus of any of the four species, he should take it to be checked.

237. What are the different levels of kashrus of the four species?

- *Mehudar* (exquisite).
- Kosher for the entire seven days (including the first day).
- Kosher for *chol hamoed*.
- *Possul* (unfit to use to fulfill the mitzvah).

238. What is *mehudar*?

Since the Torah defines the four species as *hadar* – beautiful, they can be kosher only if they are *halachically* beautiful. A species is *mehudar* if in addition, it fulfills other *halachic* specifications, which make it pleasant and beautiful in appearance and shape.

239. Why are some kosher only for *chol hamoed*?

According to the Torah, the requirement to take the four species for all seven days of Succos is only in the Temple. Outside the Temple, the Torah requires that the species be taken only on the first day. After the destruction of the Temple, the requirement to take the species everywhere was extended to all seven days of the festival. Certain conditions that are required on the first day (when the mitzvah is a Torah obligation) may not be needed on the other days.

240. What are common examples of this?

A borrowed set of species, or an incomplete esrog (see questions 389, 245 and 249). These may be used only on *chol hamoed*.

Chapter Fifteen

The Esrog

241. Does an esrog need a *hechsher*?

Yes.

242. Why does an esrog need a *hechsher*?

Since the Torah requires that the esrog be kosher to eat, it must have a *hechsher* certifying that it is not *orlah*, *tevel* etc. The *hechsher* should also certify that this fruit is not a result of grafting with another species e.g. a lemon. A grafted or non-kosher esrog may not be taken the entire seven days.

243. What else may a *hechsher* certify?

Many esrogim have a *hechsher* certifying that they may be used to fulfill the mitzvah i.e. it is complete, clean etc. The *hechsher* should be checked carefully to verify which aspects of the esrog it covers.

244. What may make an esrog *possul*?

There are three common problems that may make an esrog *possul*:
- Part of the fruit is missing.
- The pitam is missing.
- The esrog is discolored.

245. How much of the esrog must be missing to make it *possul*?

If even a tiny amount of the flesh of the esrog is missing, it is *possul*.

246. What if some of the thin layer of shiny skin is missing?

• The esrog is kosher unless the deeper green/yellow layer of the esrog is missing. However, since the outermost shiny layer is very thin, great expertise is required to verify that only this layer is missing, and it is important to confirm how deep the nick is.

• According to some opinions, the esrog is still kosher even if the green/yellow layer is missing and only *possul* when the deeper white fleshy layer is missing.

247. What if an expert is uncertain if some of the green/yellow layer is missing?

The esrog may be used.

248. What if the stem (underneath the esrog) is missing?

If the entire stem broke off leaving the stem hole completely hollow, the esrog is incomplete and *possul*. If the stem hole remains fully covered, the esrog is kosher. Some place the esrog next to apples before Succos in order to change its color from green to yellow. This may cause the stem to fall off, and an expert should be consulted before attempting to do this.

249. May a *b'racha* be recited over an incomplete esrog after the first day of Yom Tov?

- On the second day of Yom Tov in *chutz la'aretz*, one may take such an esrog and recite a *b'racha* over it if no other is available and only a tiny amount is missing. If a larger amount is missing, a *b'racha* may not be recited.

- During *chol hamoed*, one may recite a *b'racha* over it even if a large amount is missing. Preferably, a person should not recite a *b'racha* on an incomplete esrog even on *chol hamoed*.

250. What is a pitam?

The pitam is the vertical stick-like protuberance that grows out of the tip of the esrog. It is covered by a flower-like piece called a *shoshanta*.

251. Do all esrogim grow with a pitam?

Yes. Initially, all esrogim grow with a pitam. However, as the esrog develops the pitam usually dries up, shrivels and drops off. Such an esrog is kosher and is not considered to be incomplete. Only a small percentage of esrogim retain the pitam even when fully grown.

252. What if the pitam was knocked off a fully-grown esrog?

This depends on the type of pitam:
- If it is a continuous green/yellow extension of the flesh of the esrog, the esrog is incomplete and *possul*.

- If the pitam is a piece of wood that grows out of the fruit, and all of it breaks off, the esrog is *possul*. If only a part of it breaks off leaving a small amount of wood above the tip of the fruit, the esrog is kosher. However, according to some opinions even such an esrog should preferably not be used.

253. How can one tell if the pitam fell off naturally or if it was knocked off later?

When the pitam falls off naturally, it leaves behind a characteristic indentation. If the pitam fell off at a later stage, there will be no such groove. Often an expert will be able to determine the status of the esrog even if this groove is apparently absent.

254. What if the *shoshanta* fell off a fully-grown esrog?

If only the *shoshanta* came off but the entire pitam was left intact, the esrog is kosher. Nevertheless, it should be used only if it is superior in other respects to an esrog that is not missing a *shoshanta*.

255. May a person use an esrog with a missing pitam on *chol hamoed*?

- Preferably, one should not use such an esrog.
- If no other esrog is available, a person may use such an esrog without reciting a *b'racha*.

256. Which colors make an esrog *possul*?

White, black, dark brown and dark green are colors that can make an esrog *possul*. Beige is not *possul*.

257. Where on the esrog do these colors make it *possul*?

On the upper part of the esrog, one dot will make it *possul*. On the lower part of the esrog, two or more marks will make it *possul* if at least one can be seen whichever side one looks at.

258. What is regarded as the upper part of the esrog?

The section of the esrog that slopes towards the pitam.

259. Is the pitam itself included in this?

- If there is a single dot on a fleshy pitam, the esrog is *possul*.
- If there is a dot on a woody pitam, the esrog is kosher.

260. What size do these dots have to be?

The esrog is only *possul* if the dots are large enough to be seen easily by a person of average vision holding the esrog at a comfortable distance. If the dot can be seen only after close inspection or only with a magnifying glass, the esrog is kosher.

261. Is a discolored esrog kosher during *chol hamoed*?

In normal circumstances, such an esrog should not be used. However, if no other esrog is available, it may be used and a *b'racha* recited.

262. If the discoloration was cut out, may the esrog be used on *chol hamoed*?

It may be used only if no other esrog is available. This is true even though an incomplete esrog is usually kosher on *chol hamoed* (see question 249).

263. What if the dots are stuck onto the esrog but not part of it?

If the dots are only dirt, the esrog is kosher.

264. Should a person try to remove them?

They should preferably be removed to clarify that they are in fact dirt and not part of the esrog. This should be done only by an expert since the esrog could easily become *possul* by the removal of some of its flesh. Similarly, rubbing the skin of the esrog forcibly may damage the skin of the esrog.

265. What if the esrog was bruised causing a change in its color?

The esrog is kosher. This color change is caused by juice leaking onto the skin and can often be prevented by rinsing the esrog immediately after it was knocked.

266. What if an esrog develops brown marks through constant use?

Such an esrog is kosher.

267. How can a person prevent these brown marks?

When selecting an esrog, it is important to hold it gently with one's fingertips. This will help to prevent the development of brown marks during use.

268. What if the esrog has cream colored scab marks (*blettel*) on it?

These marks are a result of thorns or leaves resting on the fruit during growth.

- If the marks are white, see questions 256 and 257.
- If the marks are cream, and not raised above the skin of the esrog, the esrog is kosher but not *mehudar*.
- If the marks are cream and raised above the skin of the esrog, the esrog may be *possul* depending on the number and placing of the marks (see question 257).

269. What if some of the scab has fallen off?

- If a thorn or branch scraped out some flesh of the esrog, the presence of the scab is essential since it completes the fruit. Therefore, if such a scab falls off, the esrog is incomplete.
- If the branch merely irritated the skin causing a scab to form, the esrog is still intact and kosher even if the scab falls off.

An esrog with a scab mark should be brought to an expert to determine its status.

270. What is the minimum size of an esrog?

An esrog should have the volume of 100cc (approx. 100g). Preferably, one should buy an esrog that is larger than this, to allow for shrinkage (see question 278).

271. How can one prevent an esrog from shrinking?

It should be wrapped in a plastic/zip-lock bag and kept in a cool place. It should be aired every day (except Shabbos – see question 383).

272. What is the maximum size of the esrog?

There is no maximum size. However, the larger the esrog is, the more unlikely it is to be *mehudar* (see question 278). Additionally, a very large esrog may be difficult to hold together with the other species.

273. What color should the esrog be?

Ideally, the esrog should be yellow. One should be wary about buying an esrog that is bright yellow, since this indicates that it is over-ripe and may begin to rot.

274. Is a green esrog kosher?

Yes, but an esrog that is extremely dark green is *possul*. Preferably, one should only use a green esrog if it has begun to turn yellow (see also question 248).

275. What is the ideal shape of the esrog?

The esrog should preferably be built like a tower; widest near the base, becoming narrower towards the pitam. An esrog that is shaped like a ball is *possul*.

276. Should the pitam be directly above the stem?

It is a *hiddur* for the stem and pitam to be in line.

277. Is an esrog that is well shaped but marked more *mehudar* than one that is clean but not well shaped?

No. The clean one is more *mehudar*.

278. What makes an esrog *mehudar*?

In decreasing order of importance:

- The flesh of the esrog is certainly complete, without nicks or scratches.
- The esrog, and especially the upper section, is completely clean, including from leaf marks.
- The esrog is not too big or too small.
- The esrog is yellow.
- The stem is recessed into the esrog.
- The esrog is not smooth like a lemon but covered with characteristic bumps.
- The esrog has a pitam.
- The stem and the pitam are in line.

Chapter Sixteen
The Lulav

279. Must a lulav have a *hechsher*?
No. However, since according to one opinion some species of lulav are *possul,* one should preferably buy a lulav from a reliable supplier.

280. How should the leaves lie?
The leaves should lie flat on the spine.

281. What if the leaves fan out to the side?
The lulav is kosher if the leaves can be tied down flat onto the spine. Such a lulav is not *mehudar* (see also question 314).

282. How are the lulav leaves formed?
Each leaf is comprised of two individual leaves. These two leaves are connected along their length on the same side as the spine of the lulav and separate on the opposite side.

283. What if these two leaves are not connected?
If the leaves are separate along most of their length, the lulav may be *possul.*

284. When will the lulav be *possul*?

- If most of the leaves are split to this extent (this is extremely uncommon) **or**
- If the *teyomes* leaf is split.

285. What is the *teyomes* leaf?

The *teyomes* is the double leaf that grows out of the top of the spine. Usually, this is the tallest of all the lulav leaves.

286. To what extent should the two leaves of the *teyomes* be connected?

- A lulav is certainly *mehudar* if the *teyomes* leaves are attached for their entire length.
- A lulav is *mehudar* according to some opinions if the *teyomes* leaves are separated less than 8cm.
- A lulav is kosher if the *teyomes* leaves are attached for half their length. (See also question 300.)

287. What if this leaf isn't doubled?

The lulav is *possul*.

288. What if two double-leaves are growing out of the top of the spine?

Both of them are called *teyomes*.

289. How do the laws of a split *teyomes* apply to such a lulav?

The above laws apply to each of the two *teyomes*.

290. Why is it important that the *teyomes* be fully closed?

If the leaves are somewhat separated, the lulav can easily become *possul* if the leaves separate further when it is waved during the festival.

291. Can this separation be prevented?

Yes. If the lulav is not already *possul*, the leaves can be stuck together with adhesive to prevent them from separating. A rav should be consulted before doing this.

292. May one use a lulav with a split *teyomes* after the first day?

On the second day of Yom Tov in *chutz la'aretz* a *b'racha* may not be recited over such a lulav, but during *chol hamoed* one may recite a *b'racha* over it.

293. What if the top of the *teyomes* has been cut off?

The lulav is *possul* if any amount of leaf is missing. Similarly, if the tips are missing from most of the other leaves, the lulav is *possul* (this is rare). Some lulavim have a brown needle-like projection extending beyond the top of the *teyomes*. If this is missing, the lulav is still kosher, but an expert should be consulted to ascertain whether part of the leaf is also missing.

294. What if only one leaf of the *teyomes* has been cut off?

One should preferably not use such a lulav.

295. What if a lulav with two *teyomes* has one cut *teyomes*(see question 288)?

The lulav may be used as long as one *teyomes* is complete.

296. How can one tell if the top has been chopped off?

A complete lulav may have a tiny indentation in the top that can be identified with a magnifying glass. Even if this is not apparent, an expert will be able to determine if the lulav is incomplete.

297. After the first day, may one use a lulav whose *teyomes* has been chopped off?

No. Such a lulav is *possul* for all seven days.

298. What if the two leaves of the *teyomes* have different heights?

• According to many opinions, the lulav is kosher as long as the lower leaf reaches halfway up the taller leaf.

• According to some opinions, the lulav is kosher only if the two leaves are almost the same height.

• According to a third opinion, the leaves should be exactly the same height.

299. What if the two leaves are different widths?

The lulav is kosher if the narrower leaf covers the majority of the width of the wider leaf for its entire length.

300. What if the two leaves look separate?

If the tips of the two leaves diverge and look like two prongs of a fork the lulav is *possul*, even if the two leaves are connected for almost their entire length. Such a lulav is *possul* even if the two leaves appear only slightly apart from each other, as long as a clear gap can be seen between them.

301. Is it simple to identify this type of lulav?

No. Since such a lulav could almost be considered *mehudar* (see question 286), much expertise is required to verify if it is in fact *possul*. Great care should be taken to avoid buying such a lulav (see question 236).

302. May such a lulav be used on *chol hamoed*?

Yes.

303. What if this happened to a lulav that has two *teyomes* (see question 288)?

The lulav is *possul* even if only one *teyomes* has this fault.

304. May a person use a lulav if the leaves have a brown covering?

Yes. However, the outer leaves should be separated to allow them to rustle when the lulav is waved (see question 368). The central three leaves should not be separated.

305. Is such a lulav *mehudar*?

According to some opinions, even if the removal of the covering would reveal a split *teyomes*, the lulav is *mehudar* since the brown covering presently connects the leaves. According to other opinions, the brown covering should be removed very carefully to check the status of the *teyomes*. Many suppliers object strongly to customers removing the brown covering, and one must receive explicit permission before doing so.

306. May a person use a lulav if the tops of the leaves are wrinkled like a zigzag?

Such a lulav should be avoided if possible. In any event one should check that the top does not look like a fork, since this is very common in such a lulav (see question 300).

307. Is a dry lulav kosher?

- If most of the leaves have dried out and become very light green, the lulav is *possul*.
- If the *teyomes* has dried out, the lulav should not be used.
- If only the tip of the *teyomes* has dried out, the lulav should preferably not be used.

308. How can one prevent the lulav from becoming dried out?

In a hot climate, an unprotected lulav can become dried out and *possul* in a few hours. The lulav should be kept in a cool place, preferably sealed in an airtight plastic holder.

309. What if the tip of the lulav has become burnt by the sun?

The lulav is kosher.

310. Is a bent lulav kosher?

Yes. However, the lulav is *mehudar* only if the spine is completely straight.

311. What if the tops of the leaves are folded over?

If most of them are folded over, the lulav should not be used. If the leaves are only slightly bent, the lulav is kosher.

312. What if the *teyomes* is folded over?

If the top of the *teyomes* is folded over, the lulav is kosher. Some opinions prefer this type of lulav since the *teyomes* cannot be split.

313. How long should the lulav be?

Preferably, the length of the spine should be 40cm. This is measured from where the lowest pair of leaves are connected to the spine until the top of the spine (but not including the top leaf). A lulav whose spine measures 32cm is kosher. In extenuating circumstances, one may use a lulav if the spine measures 27cm. In any event, a short lulav should be avoided, since it is difficult to tie the hadassim and aravos to it in the correct formation (see question 353). According to one opinion, a long lulav is more *mehudar*.

314. What is a *mehudar* lulav?

In decreasing order of importance:

- The leaves of the *teyomes* are closed all the way to the top.
- The leaves lie completely flat on the spine.
- The spine of the lulav is at least 40cm long.
- The leaves of the *teyomes* are both exactly the same size.
- The lulav is green and healthy looking.
- The lulav is completely straight, like a spear.

Chapter Seventeen

The Hadas

315. What is the hadas?

The hadas is the twig from a myrtle tree.

316. How many hadassim are taken?

Three.

317. What is the ideal formation of its leaves?

The twig should be covered by sets of three leaves growing out of it along its whole length. The three leaves should be growing from the twig at the same level around its circumference.

318. What length of the hadas should have this three-leaf formation?

Ideally, the twig should have this formation for 30cm. The leaves beyond the top of the twig are not included in this measurement. The hadas is still kosher if only 24cm is like this (see also question 323).

319. When are the three leaves considered to be at the same level?

Each leaf has a stem that attaches it to the twig. If an imaginary line drawn around the twig would pass through the three stems, then the leaves are considered to be at the same level. It is not necessary for the three stems to begin at exactly the same height on the twig.

320. What if some of the leaves are growing at a different level?

Then those leaves may not be included in the required length of the hadas. If the three-leaf formation does not extend over the required length, the hadas may not be used for the entire seven days.

321. Must the required length be continuous?

Ideally yes, but if necessary one may combine several kosher sections to make up the required length.

322. What if the tips of the leaves do not reach the stem of the leaf above it along the twig?

The hadas is kosher. It is a *hiddur* to use a hadas whose leaves overlap.

323. What if some of the leaves have fallen off?

If no other twig is available, the hadas may still be used if:

• The majority of the required length (13cm) has the three-leaf formation and the rest of the twig is bare, even if the leaves at the top of the twig are missing, or this length is made up of short three-leaf sections spread out along the length of the twig **or**

• The entire length of the twig has sets of two leaves at the same level.

Care should be taken not to detach any leaves when tying the hadassim to the lulav (see question 352).

324. What if part of a leaf is missing?

The leaf is regarded as complete if most of it remains. If the majority is missing, see previous question.

325. What if the leaves are slit?

The twig is kosher if most of the leaves are complete and intact.

326. What if additional small twigs and leaves are growing together with the sets of three leaves?

Since these leaves disturb the three-leaf formation, they should preferably be carefully removed.

327. Is a dry hadas kosher?

A hadas that has lost all its color is *possul*. This is extremely uncommon in hadassim that were cut that year.

328. What if the top of the twig is missing?

Such a hadas should preferably not be used.

329. How should the hadassim be kept fresh during Succos?

They can be stood in a small amount of water, or kept in an airtight bag in a cool place. Many keep them in the refrigerator in a sealed bag with a few drops of water (but care must be taken to ensure that the refrigerator is not ice cold).

330. May one put the hadassim in water on Yom Tov?

If they were in water before Yom Tov, they may be returned to the same water on Yom Tov. More water may be added on Yom Tov but the water may not be changed until *chol hamoed*.

331. What is a *mehudar* hadas?

In decreasing order of importance:

• The twig has the three-leaf formation for at least 30cm of its length up to the top and all the leaves are complete.

• The leaves are all green and look fresh.

• The leaves should lie flat on the twig, not point out at an angle.

• The leaves should be no larger than a thumbnail.

• The top of one leaf reaches the bottom of the leaf that is above it along the twig.

Chapter Eighteen

The Aravah

332. What is the aravah?

The aravah is the twig from a willow tree.

333. How many aravos are taken?

Two.

334. How is the aravah best identified?

The aravah has three characteristic features:
- The leaves are long and narrow
- The leaves have smooth edges
- The twig is usually red.

Care should be taken not to confuse the willow tree with the eucalyptus tree that has similar features. The eucalyptus tree can be identified by its fragrance, whereas the willow has no smell.

335. What if the edges of the leaves are not smooth?

The twig is kosher if the edges of the leaves are slightly serrated, provided that they are long and the twig is red. The aravos commonly available in *Eretz Yisrael* all have slightly serrated edges.

336. What if the edges of the leaves are very jagged?

This type of willow is usually missing all three characteristics. The leaves are typically wide and the twig is pale green. Such a twig should be avoided.

337. What if the twig is not red?

The twig is still kosher if it is green, as long as it would turn red if left in the sun. An aravah with a white twig is *possul*.

338. Should it grow by a river?

According to some opinions, it is preferable that the twigs come from a tree that grows next to a river.

339. How long should the aravah be?

Ideally, the twig should be 30cm long, but it is still kosher if it measures only 24cm. The twig should be measured between the stems of the lowest and highest leaves.

340. What if some of the leaves are missing?

The aravah is kosher if most of them are present along the required length. Care should be taken not to detach any leaves when tying the aravos to the lulav (see question 352). However, since aravos are easily available, one should only use those that have all their leaves (see question 345).

341. What if the leaves are incomplete?

The leaf is regarded as complete if most of it remains. If the majority is missing, see question 340.

342. What if the leaves are split?

If the majority are split, the twig is *possul*. Similarly, if most of the leaves are only partially connected at their stem, the twig is *possul*.

343. What if the leaves are wilted or pointing downwards?

If most of the leaves have dried out and lost all their color, the twig is *possul*. If the leaves only point downwards (as is common), the aravah is kosher. It is praiseworthy to change the aravos for fresh ones whenever possible.

344. What if the top of the twig is missing?

If the twig is incomplete, the aravah is *possul*. It is kosher only if the twig is complete, even if the top leaf is incomplete (but see question 340).

345. Is it better for the twig to be topped by a complete leaf?

Some prefer this type of aravah, since it confirms that the twig is in fact complete. This is commonly called '*lavluv*'.

346. What is a *mehudar* aravah?

In descending order of importance:
- The stem is 30cm long.

- The leaves are all green, look fresh and are complete.
- The leaves are long and have smooth edges.
- The stem is red.
- The stem is topped by a complete leaf.
- They come from a tree that grows next to a river.

Chapter Nineteen

Tying the Species

347. Must the species be tied together?

There is no obligation to tie the species together, but it is a mitzvah and the custom to do so, thereby beautifying the mitzvah.

348. Which of the species should be tied together?

The lulav, hadassim and aravos should be tied together. The lulav should be in the center with the spine facing the person, the three hadassim should be tied to the right of the lulav and the two aravos tied to the left.

349. How should a left-handed person position them?

The same way, i.e. hadassim on the right of the lulav etc. (but see question 359).

350. With what should one tie the species?

Although they may be tied with any material, the custom is to use lulav leaves. A person can remove an outer leaf from his own lulav (on condition that this does not render his lulav *possul* - see question 313), split it and use it like string.

351. How should the lulav be tied?

The lulav itself should be tied in three places. The uppermost ring should be at least 8cm below the top of the spine to allow the leaves to rustle when it is waved (see also questions 368, 304).

352. How should the other species be tied to the lulav?

•   The three species should be tied together using a double knot. According to some opinions, this knot is one of the three that the lulav is tied with. According to other opinions, this is an additional knot. Some have the custom to tie them together with two additional knots, making a total of five knots.

•   Many have the custom to bind the species together using a braided lulav-leaf receptacle. Nevertheless, it is preferable to wrap a lulav string higher than this receptacle and tie a double-knot.

In any event, extreme care should be taken not to pull off any leaves from the hadassim or aravos when tying them to the lulav.

353. How should the species be positioned?

The spine of the lulav should extend at least 8cm above the tips of the hadas twigs. Also, the tips of the hadas twigs should extend slightly above the tips of the aravos twigs.

354. When should the species be tied together?

The species must be tied before the first day of Succos since it is forbidden to tie a double knot on Yom Tov. When the first day of Yom Tov is on Shabbos (and the species are not taken), the species may be tied on *motzai* Shabbos.

355. Who should tie the species together?

Preferably, a Jewish man should tie the species. If a woman, child or gentile tied them, they should be tied again if possible.

356. What if the species were not tied before Yom Tov?

The custom is to wrap the leaf around the three species and tuck it in, without tying it. After Yom Tov, the leaf should be retied with a double knot. If necessary, one may even detach a leaf from the lulav on Yom Tov for this purpose. However, if the lulav has already been used for the mitzvah, some opinions forbid the use of its leaves for tying the species (see question 415).

Chapter Twenty

Taking the Species

357. When should the species be taken?

The main custom is to take them in shul immediately before reciting *hallel*. Others have the custom to take them in the succah before *shacharis* provided it is after sunrise.

358. How are the species taken?

The lulav, hadassim and aravos should first be picked up in the right hand, with their tips pointing up and the spine of the lulav facing the person. Then, the esrog should be picked up in the left hand with the upper tip pointing **down**.

359. How should a left-handed person take them?

A left-handed person should take the three species in his left hand, and the esrog in his right hand.

360. What if a person took the species in the opposite hands?

He should switch the species as soon as he realizes. If he has already recited the *b'racha*, he need not repeat it.

361. What if all the species were taken in one hand?

He should hold the species correctly as soon as he realizes. If he has already recited the *b'racha*, he need not repeat it.

362. Why is the esrog picked up inverted?

Strictly speaking, one fulfills the mitzvah of 'taking' the four species by simply picking them up. By doing so, one would not be able to recite the *b'racha* as one should before the mitzvah is fulfilled. Since the mitzvah is only fulfilled when the species are held upright (in the manner in which they grow), the esrog should be picked up with the tip pointing down. The *b'racha* is recited, the esrog turned the right way up, placed next to the other species and then the species waved. On the first day when two *brachos* are recited, the esrog should not be turned the right way up until both *brachos* have been recited. Similarly, when taking the species from another person to fulfill the mitzvah, one should be careful to receive the esrog inverted. Alternatively, the *b'racha* could be recited when holding only the three species in the right hand, and the esrog picked up after reciting the *b'racha*.

363. What if a person picked up the esrog with the tip pointing up?

The *b'racha* may nevertheless be recited.

364. What if a person waved the species with the esrog inverted?

He should turn the esrog the right way up and wave the species again. If he has already put the species down, he must repeat the *b'racha* before taking them again. He should still follow the procedure outlined in question 362.

365. Which *b'racha* is recited?

On the first day that the species are taken, two *brachos* are recited:

• אשר קדשנו במצותיו וצונו על נטילת לולב.

• שהחיינו.

On subsequent days, only the first *b'racha* is recited (even in *chutz la'aretz*).

366. What if a person forgot to recite the *shehecheyanu b'racha* on the first day?

• If the *hoshanos* have not yet been performed, he may still recite the *shehecheyanu b'racha*.

• If the *hoshanos* have been performed, the *shehecheyanu b'racha* should be recited on the following day when the species are taken.

367. How many times is the *b'racha* recited?

The *b'racha* over the species is recited once a day. Even if a person takes a different set of species, the *b'racha* may not be repeated. In circumstances when a person's set proved to be completely unfit to fulfill the mitzvah, the *b'racha* must be repeated on a kosher set.

368. How are the species waved?

While the three species are held in the right hand and the esrog next to them in the left, the species are waved around the body. Each wave is made by extending the arms away from the body and returning the species back to the chest. The lulav should be waved gently so that the leaves rustle against each other during each wave.

369. In which directions are the species waved?

The species are waved in six directions; forwards, to the right, behind, left, up and down.

370. How many times are the species waved?

The species are waved three times in each direction, i.e. three times forwards, three times to the right etc.

371. Why are the species waved in different directions?

- They are waved in four directions to the One who owns the four directions, and up and down to the One who owns heaven and earth. This is a declaration that all existence depends on Hashem, who created and maintains the entire universe.
- They are waved in four directions to prevent harmful winds, and up and down to ward off harmful dews. On Succos, Hashem judges the world for rains, and the four species are especially dependent upon water. By waving them we pray for abundant rains that will not be hindered by harmful rains or dews.

372. Should a person turn and face each direction when waving the species?

No. A person should stand facing forwards and point the tips of the species in the different directions that the species are waved. The species are waved behind over the shoulder. (In a confined space, care should be taken not to cause any injury to other congregants or to the tip of the lulav.) Some have the custom to turn around while waving the species in the different directions.

373. How are the species waved in the downward direction?

The tips are not pointed in the downward direction, since they would then not be held in the manner in which they grew (see question 362). Rather, with the tips pointing upwards, the species are waved towards the ground.

374. May one speak after waving the species?

If the species are taken immediately before *hallel*, it is praiseworthy not to speak until after *hallel*, so that the *b'racha* can apply to the waving during *hallel*.

375. When are the species taken during *davening*?

- Before *hallel* according to the main custom (see question 357).
- During *hallel*.
- During *hoshanos*.

376. How are the species held during *hallel* and *hoshanos*?

They should be held in two hands, with all four species in constant contact (see question 404).

377. When are the species waved during *hallel*?

- During the verse הודו לה' כי טוב, which is recited a total of six times.
- During the verse אנא ה' הושיעה נא, which is repeated.

378. How are the species waved during the verse הודו לה' כי טוב?

The species are not waved when saying the name of Hashem. They are waved forwards three times while saying the first word, הודו, held still while reciting the name of Hashem, to the right three times for the third word כי, behind for the fourth word טוב etc. This procedure is done in total six times; four when reciting the verse in response to the chazan and twice again when this verse is recited towards the end of *hallel*.

379. Does the chazan do the same?

No. He waves the species only when reciting the first two verses, הודו and יאמר נא ישראל (one direction for each word). He does not wave them when reciting the verses that begin יאמרו נא.

380. How are the species waved during the verse אנא ה' הושיעה נא?

The species are waved in two directions at each word (three times in each direction) but not when reciting the name of Hashem. Some have the custom to wave in a different direction at each syllable, i.e. in two directions at the word אנא, in three directions at the word הושיעה and in one direction at the word נא.

381. What if a person is *davening* alone?

He waves the species when reciting the verse כי הודו לה' טוב (a total of three times) and when reciting the repeated verse אנא ה' הושיעה נא.

382. How should the species be put down?

In the reverse order from how they were picked up, i.e. the esrog should be put down first.

383. Are the species taken on Shabbos?

The species are taken on all the days of Succos, with the exception of Shabbos. Even if the first day of Succos is on Shabbos (when there is a Torah obligation to take the species), they are not taken. All four species are *muktzeh* on Shabbos and cannot be moved.

384. Why are the species not taken on Shabbos?

The Sages forbade taking the four species on Shabbos lest one accidentally carry them in a street where there is no *eiruv*. For the same reason, we do not blow the *shofar* or read the *megillah* on Shabbos.

385. Should a woman remove her rings before taking the species?

Yes, since no item may intervene between the hands and the species. Similarly, men who wear *tefillin* on *chol hamoed* should remove them before taking the species. Care should also be taken to remove all the flax in which the esrog is wrapped.

386. What if a person forgot to remove rings, *tefillin* etc?

The species should be taken again but the *b'racha* not repeated.

387. What if a person has a bandage on his hand?

The bandage does not need to be removed. According to some opinions, it is preferable to hold the species between the fingers (if they are not bandaged).

Chapter Twenty-one

Acquiring the Species

388. Must every man own a set of four species?

On the first day of Succos (and the second in *chutz la'aretz*), a person can only fulfill the mitzvah with a set that he owns. It is therefore preferable that every man buys a set for himself. (See question 392.)

389. May one buy the species on credit?

Ideally, the species should be purchased with cash or a check, but not on credit.

390. Can a post-dated check be used?

Preferably, the check should be payable before Succos. If a down payment is given before Succos, the species can certainly be used.

391. May one purchase any of the species from a child?

This should be avoided. According to some opinions, a person cannot make a full acquisition on articles purchased from a child, and such species would be invalid for the first day of Succos (and the second in *chutz la'aretz*). This is especially relevant to aravos that are often sold by children. According to some opinions, this applies in certain cases even when the seller is over bar mitzvah but is financially dependent on his parents.

392. What if a man does not own a set?

Another person should give him his set as a present, stipulating a condition that they are to be returned after use.

393. What if the species were not returned?

Since the condition was not fulfilled, the person who borrowed them has not fulfilled his obligation. The same is true if the species were returned *possul*.

394. Can a person fulfill his obligation with species that he received with no specification?

Yes. We assume that they were given so that he would be able to fulfill his obligation and the condition is self-understood.

395. Can the borrower give the species to someone else?

Yes, but the next borrower should preferably receive explicit permission from the owner. They may not be given to anyone else if the original owner stipulated so. Also, if the owner would be unhappy about many people taking his species out of concern that they may be damaged, they may not be passed around even if he did not make an explicit stipulation.

396. Should a person make a *b'racha* on another person's *mehudar* set or his own kosher set?

On the first day (and the second day in *chutz la'aretz*), he should use his own kosher set. During *chol hamoed* he may use either set.

397. May a person give his species to a child?

Since a child is *halachically* unable to return the species once he has acquired them, he should not be given them at all on the first day (and the second in *chutz la'aretz*). Even after the owner has fulfilled his own obligation, he should not give them to a child, since he will then be unable to give his set to another adult who may need to fulfill his obligation.

398. How can a child fulfill his obligation?

• Preferably, a father should purchase a kosher set of species for his boys under bar mitzvah. For this purpose, species that are minimally kosher are sufficient and it is unnecessary to buy a *mehudar* set. (One should certainly endeavor to buy sets for sons over bar mitzvah.)

• Alternatively, according to some opinions a child can be lent the species and fulfill his mitzvah even though they do not belong to him. This is the common custom.

399. At what age should a child be trained to take the species?

When he knows how to wave them (see question 368). This is usually around six or seven.

400. Are women obligated to wave the four species?

No. Women are exempt from this mitzvah since it is a positive mitzvah bound by time.

401. Is it praiseworthy for women to take the species?

Yes. According to *Ashkenazic* custom, women may even recite the *b'racha* over the species. They must be careful on the first day (and second day in *chutz la'aretz*) to receive the species as a gift.

Chapter Twenty-two

Hoshanos

402. What are *hoshanos*?

When the Temple stood, huge willow branches were brought and leaned against the altar during Succos. The *shofar* was blown and the Cohanim would walk around the altar and recite the prayer '*hosha na'* - Please bring salvation. Then the people would come in and wave the aravos. On the seventh day of Succos (the last day of *chol hamoed*), these branches were brought even if it was Shabbos, and the altar was encircled seven times. To remember this mitzvah, we walk around the *bimah* once each day and seven times on the seventh day of Succos (*Hoshanah Rabbah*).

403. What is the procedure for *hoshanos*?

The Ark is opened and one of the congregants removes a *sefer* Torah and holds it at the *bimah*. The introductory four verses are recited, and anyone who has a set of species holds them while standing still. While reciting the following paragraph the congregation circles the *bimah* counter-clockwise once, holding the species in two hands.

404. Is it permitted to hold the species in one hand?

In order to hold a siddur, many hold all four species in the right hand. However, if at all possible, it is preferable to hold them in two hands. The siddur can be balanced on the arms, or a lightweight copy used which can be held easily between the fingers.

405. What if a person does not have his own set of species?

Only those who are holding a set of four species should walk around the *bimah*.

406. Who should hold the *sefer* Torah if everyone holds a set of species?

- If there is a mourner, he should hold the *sefer* Torah (see next question).
- If there is no mourner, someone should offer to hold the *sefer* Torah instead of circling the *bimah*. It is a greater mitzvah to hold the *sefer* Torah than to circle the *bimah*.

407. Does a mourner walk around the *bimah*?

No, but he may stand at the *bimah* holding a *sefer* Torah. It is a mitzvah for him to give his set of species to someone who does not own a set, to enable him to walk around the *bimah*.

408. How are the *hoshanos* recited on Shabbos?

The ark is opened and the prayers are recited standing still, without taking the four species (see question 383).

409. What is the special significance of *Hoshanah Rabbah*?

On Succos, Hashem passes judgement on rainfall and additional prayers are said on this day to seal a favorable verdict. Additionally, it says in the *Zohar* that on this day all the decrees that were sealed on Yom Kippur are dispatched. An unfavorable sentence can still be torn up through a sincere repentance. There is a widespread custom to read the entire book of *Devarim* in shul on the evening of *Hoshanah Rabbah*, and some remain awake the whole night to study Torah.

410. What changes to prayer are made on *Hoshanah Rabba*?

• Many sections of *davening* are recited with the tune that is used on Rosh Hashanah and Yom Kippur.

• The chazzan or other congregants may have a custom to wear a *kittel*.

• The *pesukei d'zimra* which is usually reserved for Shabbos and Yom Tov is recited, including *mizmor lesodah* (psalm 100) and *mizmor shir l'yom haShabbos* (psalm 92). The prayer *nishmas* is not recited.

• The *sefer* Torah is removed from the ark using the prayers usually recited on Yom Tov, and the thirteen attributes of mercy are recited.

- The *kedushah* recited during *mussaf* is the one usually recited on Shabbos.

411. What other changes are made during *davening*?

- All the *sifrei* Torah are removed from the Ark when encircling the *bimah* seven times with the four species.
- Some of the rings around the lulav are removed, enabling the leaves to be rustled more effectively.
- A bundle of aravah twigs is taken.

412. May one use the aravos from the lulav bundle?

If one removes them from the lulav bundle, they may be used for this mitzvah. However, after they have been used, they may no longer be kosher to use in the lulav bundle. This should be taken into consideration if any other people may need to wave the lulav.

413. How many twigs are taken?

It is sufficient to take three but most have the custom to take five.

414. Which twig is kosher for this mitzvah?

Whatever is kosher for the aravah in the four species is also kosher for this mitzvah. In extenuating circumstances, it is sufficient to take one twig even if it only has one leaf. It is a *hiddur* to use long twigs.

415. How are these twigs tied together?

The custom is to tie them with a lulav leaf or willow twig. According to some opinions, one may not use a leaf from the lulav that has been taken during Succos. If one has neither a lulav leaf nor a willow twig, one may tie the bundle with string or an elastic band, but the bundle should not be held at this place.

416. What is done with the twigs?

The twigs are waved in the same manner as the four species (see question 368) but no *b'racha* is recited. Some have the custom to wave them just a little. Additionally, they are beaten on the ground.

417. When is this bundle taken?

After the *bimah* has been encircled seven times with the four species, before the paragraph beginning תענה אמונים.

418. When should the *aravah* bundle be beaten?

At the end of the prayers, during or after the triple recitation of the words קול מבשר מבשר ואומר. Some have the custom to beat it after the chazan has recited *kaddish*.

419. How many times are they beaten?

The bundle should be beaten five times on the ground. Preferably, they should be hit afterwards against a chair or any suitable object to remove some of the leaves, but not all the leaves have to be removed.

420. Can many people use the same *aravah* bundle?

The custom is to endeavor to obtain a separate bundle for each person, but if necessary several people may use the same bundle.

421. What should be done with the aravos after they have been used?

Some have the custom to put the twigs on top of the ark, while others challenge that this is disrespectful. In any event, they should be disposed of respectfully and many use it for another *mitzva* (see question 422).

422. What should be done with the species after Succos?

They should be treated with respect and not disposed of in the regular garbage (see question 205). It is praiseworthy to use them for another mitzvah and many have the custom to use them as fuel in the fire when baking matzos or when burning the chometz on *erev* Pesach. It is permitted to use the esrog to make jelly.

Appendix: Halachic Measurements

Throughout this book, reference is made to various halachic measurements, e.g. *tefachim*, *kezayis*, *kebeitza* etc. Although there is much controversy about these measurements, the two most widely accepted opinions are those of HaRav Chaim Naeh and the *Chazon Ish*. According to the *Mishnah B'rura* (Chapter 486) one should use a stricter measurement when the issue involves a Torah mitzvah and one may use a lenient measurement when the issue involves a Rabbinic mitzvah.

It is worth noting that sometimes the smaller measurement is the stricter. In addition, there are slight variations within each opinion and the figures given are approximate. When the measurments of one's succah or four species are very close to these figures, a rav should be consulted.

	R' Chaim Naeh	Chazon Ish	See Questions
1 tefach	8cm	10cm	84, 286, 351, 353
3 tefachim	24cm	30cm	31, 33, 45, 318, 339
4 tefachim	32cm	40cm	10, 61, 232, 313
7 tefachim	56cm	70cm	19, 22, 43, 48
10 tefachim	80cm	1m	21, 24, 31, 32, 96
1 amah	48cm	58cm	27
4 amos	1.92m	2.3m	48
1 kezayis	29cc	50cc	79,102-104, 159-161, 175
1 kebeitza	58cc	100cc	79, 81, 102, 103, 113, 162, 163, 270

Glossary

Amah (pl. *amos*) - Cubit (see appendix).

Ashkenaz - West European Jewry.

Bein hashmashos - *Halachic* twilight.

Bensch - To recite grace after meals.

Bimah - Table upon which the Torah is placed when reading.

B'racha (pl. *brachos*) - A blessing.

Chagim - Festival days.

Chol hamoed - The intermediate days of the festival.

Chometz - Leaven, which may not be owned or eaten during Pesach.

Chutz La'aretz - The Diaspora.

Daven - To pray.

Devarim - The book of Deuteronomy.

Eiruv - Enclosure of a public domain which transfers it into a private one in order to permit objects to be carried on *Shabbos*.

Eretz Yisrael - The land of Israel.

Erev Shabbos - The day before Shabbos.

Erev Yom Tov - The day before Yom Tov.

Gan Eden - The garden of Eden.

Haftorah - Public reading from Prophets.

Halacha (pl. *halachos*) - Jewish law.

Hallel - Psalms of Praise recited on festive days.

Hamotzi - The blessing made over bread before it is eaten (lit. 'who takes bread out of the ground').

Hashem - G-d.

Havdalah - Prayer recited at the conclusion of Shabbos and Yom Tov to divide between a holy day and a weekday.

Hechsher - Rabbinical supervision.

Hiddur - Beautification.

Hoshana Rabbah - The seventh day of Succos.

Isru chag - The day after the conclusion of the Yom Tov.

Kaddish - Part of congregational prayer.

Kashrus - Matters concerning Kosher items.

Kebeitza - A volume measure (see appendix).

Kedushah - Section of repeated *Shemoneh Esrei.*

Kezayis - A volume measure (see appendix).

Kiddush - Sanctification of *Shabbos* and *Yom Tov,* usually recited over a cup of wine.

Kittel - White outer garment.

Lashon Harah - Evil talk or slander.

Ma'ariv - The evening prayer.

Machzor - The prayer book containing the special order of prayers for festive days.

Megillah - Scroll.

Mehudar - Beautiful.

Mezonos - Food (except bread) made from primary grains.

Mezuzah (pl. *mezuzos*) - Parchment scroll on which parts of the Torah (including the *Shema*) are written. The scroll is attached to the doorway of every room.

Midrash - Commentary on the Bible.

Mincha - The afternoon prayer.

Minyan - Quorum of men required for communal prayer.

Mishnah B'rura - The classic and accepted *halachic* work on the daily and holiday laws written by Rav Yisroel Meir HaCohen Kagan (1839-1933).

Mitzvah (pl. *Mitzvos*) - A commandment.

Mizmor lesodah - Psalm 100, usually recited during *pesukei d'zimra.*

Moshe Rabbeinu - Moses our teacher.

Motzai Shabbos - The day after Shabbos.

Motzai Yom Kippur - The day after Yom Kippur.

Muktzeh - Item that may not be moved on Shabbos or Yom Tov.

Nagel vasser - Ritual washing of the hands performed upon awakening.

Nishmas - Concluding prayer of *pesukei d'zimra*, recited only on Shabbos and Yom Tov.

Orlah - Third year produce of fruit trees which is forbidden.

Pesach - Passover.

Pesukei d'zimra - Verse of praise recited at the beginning of *shacharis.*

Pidyon haben - Redemption of the firstborn.

Posek - *Halachic* authority.

Possul - Unfit.

Rav - Rabbi.

S'chach - The roof of the succah.

Sefer (pl. *sefarim*) - Jewish book(s).

Sefer Torah (pl. *Sifrei Torah*) - Hand written scroll of the five books of Moses.

Shacharis - The morning prayer.

Shehecheyanu - The blessing made to thank *Hashem* for bringing us to the time when we can benefit from a new item or perform a new mitzvah.

Sheimos - Used holy documents that must be buried.

Shemini Atzeres - The eighth day of Succos.

Shofar - Ram's horn blown at the New Year.

Siddur - Prayer book.

Simchas Torah - The last day of Succos.

Siyum - Festive meal made at the conclusion of a tractate etc.

Succos - Feast of Tabernacles.

Tamei - Spiritually impure.

Tefach (pl. *tefachim*) - Handbreadth (see appendix).

Tefillin - Phylacteries.

Tevel - Untithed produce of *Eretz Yisrael*.

Vayikra - The book of Leviticus.

Yom Tov - Festival.

Zohar - The Kabbalistic work containing secrets of the Torah, authored by Rabbi *Shimon bar Yochai* (circa 120 c.e.).

Index

A

C

E

T

U

W

Hebrew Sources

פרק א - בניית הסוכה

[1] רמ"א סו"ס תרכד וס' תרכה, מ"ב שם סק"ב, ושע"ת שם. [2] מ"ב שם, מט"א סו"ס תרכד. [3] מ"ב שם, ביכור"י סק"ה, וע' מ"ב ס' רנא סק"ג. [4] ס' תרלז סע' א ומ"ב שם, ביה"ל שם, הגרמ"פ זצ"ל הובא בספר הלכות חול המועד בפסקי הלכות אות כא. [5] ביכור"י ס' תרלה סק"ב, קצש"ע ס' קלד סע' א, אלף המגן סו"ס תרכד, פסקי תשובות ס' תרלה הע' 6 בשם החיד"א. [6] ביכור"י שם, ביה"ל ריש ס' יד, ס' תרלה סע' א, ס' תרלו מ"ב סק"ד. [7] ס' תרכו סע' א, ס' תרכח סע' א. [8] ס' תרלב סע' א. [9] מקראי קודש ס' כג, סוכה כהלכתה פ"ה, סע' ו, אות 3 בשם גדולי ההוראה. [10] מקראי קודש ס' כד, מנחת שלמה ס' צא אות יט, קונטרס מבית לוי תשרי תשנ"ג עמ' כג סע' יח. [11] מ"ב ס' תרלז סק"י וביה"ל שם, סוכה כהלכתה פ"ג, סע' א, אות 3. [12] סוכה כהלכתה פ"ג, סע' א, אות 2. [13] מ"ב ס' תרל סק"ד. [14] סוכה כהלכתה פ"ג, סע' ב, אות 1. [15] פמ"ג מש"ז ס' תרמג ד"ה אמר, ס' שלז סע' ב. [16] רמ"א ס' שלו סע' ג. [17] ע' מקורות 90. [18] מ"ב ס' תרכו סק"ק כא.

פרק ב - הסוכה

[19] ס' תרלד סע' א ומ"ב שם. [20] מ"ב סק"א. [21] הגרשז"א הובא בספר הסוכה השלם עמ' תמג, שבט הלוי ח"ח ס' קמד. [22] ס' תרלד סע' ב. [23] סע' א. [24] ס' תרלג סע' ח, עיין נספח. [25] סע' ט. [26] שם. [27] סע' א. [28] אלף המגן ס' תרכו סע' א, קו"א סק"ב, ס' תרמ שעה"צ סק"נ. [29] ס' תרל סע' א. [30] סע' י, מ"ב סק"נ. [31] שם, חזו"א ס' עז סק"ו. [32] סע' ט, מ"ב ס' תרלו סק"ד. [33] שם.

פרק ג - הסכך

[34] ס' תרכט סע' א, יד-יח. [35] אלף המגן ס' תרכו סע' יב, ס' בן איש חי שנה א פ' האזינו בהקדמה. [36] רמ"א סע' יב, סע' יד, ביכור"י תוס' ביכורים סו"ס תרכז, מקראי קודש ס' ח. [37] רמ"א ס' תרלו סע' ג, ומ"ב ס"ק יא. [38] ס' תרכט מ"ב ס"ק מט, ס' סוכה השלם עמ' רפא. [39] סע' ב, ערוה"ש סע'

ה, מנחת שלמה סי׳ כב, צי״א חי״ג ס׳ סו, מקראי קודש ס׳ יד,
שבה״ל ח״ג ס׳ צה, קהלות יעקב ס׳ יט.   [40] סע״ו.   [41] ס׳
תרלא סע׳ א.   [42] סע׳ ב, מ״ב סק״ב.   [43] מ״ב סק״ד.
[44] סע׳ ג ובמ״ב.   [45] ס׳ תרלב סע׳ ב, מ״ב סק״י, יב.   [46]
מ״ב ס״ק טו.   [47] סע׳ א.   [48] שם.   [49] ס׳ תרכט מ״ב
ס״ק כב.   [50] סע׳ ח ובמ״ב, מקראי קודש ס׳ כא.   [51] מ״ב
ס״ק כו, שו״ת בצל החכמה ח״ה ס׳ מד.   [52] רמ״א סו״ס
תרלה, מ״ב סק״י, שו״ת מי נוח ס׳ יח הובא בפסקי תשובות
אות ג הע׳ 15.   [53] רמ״א ס׳ תרכו סע׳ ב, ג, שעה״צ ס״ק כו,
מט״א ס׳ תרכה סע׳ כט.   [54] מט״א שם.   [55] עיין מקורות
6.   [56] מ״ב ס׳ תרלה סק״א, כה״ח ס׳ תרכה ס״ק יא.

פרק ד - קישוטי הסוכה

[57] שבת קלג/ב, מ״ב ס׳ תרלח ס״ק יא, ביכור״י סק״ט, שו״ת
הרשב״א ח״א ס׳ נה.   [58] תשובות והנהגות ח״ב ס׳ שז.
[59] קונטרס מבית לוי תשרי תשנ״ג עמ׳ כו סע׳ כו, שערים
מצויינים בהלכה ס׳ קלד קו״א סע׳ יב בשם שו״ת חתם סופר
ס׳ מב.   [60] מ״ב ס״ק כד, ביכור״י ס״ק יח בשם הש״ך ביו״ד.
[61] רמ״א סו״ס תרכז ומ״ב ס״ק טו, מ״ב ס׳ תרלח ס״ק יא.
[62] ס׳ הסוכה השלם עמ׳ שסא.   [63] לקט יושר עמוד קמד
עניין ב.

פרק ה - קדושת הסוכה

[64] טור ושו״ע ס׳ תרכה, רבינו בחיי ויקרא כ״ג, מג.   [65]
טור שם, גר״א שה״ש פ״א פסוק ד, ילקוט שמעוני פ׳ אמור
רמז תרנג.   [66] סוכה כח/ב, שו״ע ס׳ תרלט סע׳ א.   [67]
הגרשז״א הובא בס׳ סוכה השלם עמ׳ תנא.   [68] ס׳ תרלט
סע׳ ב, ג.   [69] ס׳ תרמ סע׳ א, מ״ב סק״א. ואע״פ שאף הן היו
באותו הנס, מ״מ מיעטן התורה בפירוש (ויקרא פכ״ג, פסוק
מב) ע׳ סוכה כח/א, פרמ״ג מש״ז סק״א, חת״ס ס׳ קפה.   [70]
כה״ח סק״ה, תורה תמימה ויקרא פכ״ג פסוק מב אות קסט,
וע׳ רמ״א ס׳ תרלט סוס״ע ב.   [71] עיין מקורות 130.   [72]
שש״כ פמ״ג סע׳ טו.   [73] ס׳ תרמ סע׳ ב.   [74] גר״ז סע׳ ד,
ערוה״ש סע׳ ב.   [75] סע׳ ד, מ״ב ס״ק כח, כט.   [76] מ״ב
סק״ל.   [77] שעה״צ סק״ד.

פרק ו - אכילה בסוכה

[78] ס׳ תרלט סע׳ ב.   [79] שם וביה״ל ד״ה כביצה מפת, ס׳
סוכה השלם עמ׳ שצה.   [80] מ״ב ס״ק טו, שעה״צ ס״ק לט.
[81] מ״ב שם.   [82] שעה״צ ס״ק כט, מקראי קודש עמ׳ קמ.
[83] ס׳ תרלד סע׳ ד, שעה״צ סק״ז.   [84] מ״ב ס״ק ו, שעה״צ
סק״ו.

פרק ז - שינה בסוכה

[85] רש״י רפ״ב דסוכה, שו״ע ס׳ תרלט סע׳ ב, טור ס׳ תרלט
בשם ר״ת, ביכור״י ס׳ תרלב סק״א.   [86] רמ״א ס׳ תרלט סע׳
ב, מ״ב ס״ק יח.   [87] מ״ב ס״ק יז, יח, ספר סוכה השלם עמ׳
תכז, פרמ״ג מש״ז ס״ק יג, של״ה.   [88] מ״ב סו״ס רלט, מעשה
רב אות רכא.   [89] כה״ח ס״ק יג.   [90] ס׳ תרמ סע׳ ד
ברמ״א, מ״ב ס״ק יט, כ, שעה״צ ס״ק כה.   [91] שערי תשובה
ריש ס׳ תרלט.   [92] ס׳ תרמ מ״ב ס״ק כז.   [93] ס׳ תרמ סע׳
ד ברמ״א, מ״ב ס״ק כו, כח, כט.   [94] מועדים וזמנים ח״א ס׳
פז, ציו״א ח״ח ס׳ כב, קונטרס מבית לוי תשרי תשנ״ג עמ׳ כז
סע׳ לה, וכולם תמהו על המ״ב ס׳ תרמ ס״ק כז.   [95] ס׳
תרכז סע׳ א, ספר סוכה השלם עמ׳ שס.   [96] שו״ת שבט
הלוי ח״ז ס׳ לו, ח״ח ס׳ קמג.   [97] ס׳ תרלט סע׳ ב, מ״ב ס״ק
יא.   [98] ביכור״י ס״ק לד, קונטרס מבית לוי תשרי תשנ״ג עמ׳
כז סע׳ לו, בן איש חי ח״א האזינו סק״ח.   [99] ס׳ תרלט סע׳
ז, מ״ב ס״ק מג.   [100] עיין מקורות 168.

פרק ח - ליל א׳ של סוכות

[101] ס׳ תרלט סע׳ ג, מ״ב ס״ק יט.   [102] מ״ב ס״ק כב, ס׳
תפו סק״א.   [103] ביה״ל ד״ה ולא יאכל וכו׳ בשם פרמ״ג.
[104] ס׳ תרלט סע׳ ג ברמ״א, מ״ב ס״ק כה.   [105] מ״ב ס״ק
כב, שיעורין של תורה שיעורי המצוות אות ל, וע׳ מט״א ס׳
תרכה ס״ק נב שחידש שלמצוה מן המובחר יש לבלוע כזית
בב״א כמו במצה, כה״ח סק״ח.   [106] נשמת אברהם ס׳ תרלט
אות ד בשם הגרשז״א, שו״ת יחוה דעת ח״ד ס׳ לז להקל, אבל
צי״א חט״ו ס׳ לב אות יג ומועו״ז ח״א ס׳ פו החמירו.   [107]
מ״ב ס׳ תרכה סק״א.   [108] מ״ב שם, ביכור״י סק״ג.   [109]
בן איש חי שנה א׳ האזינו סק״ז, מנח״ש ח״א ס׳ א.   [110]
מ״ב ס׳ תרלט ס״ק כז.   [111] עיין מקורות 157.

פרק ט - ברכת הסוכה

[112] גמ' סוכה מו/א. [113] מ"ב ס' תרלט ס"ק יג. [114] שם ס"ק טז. [115] מ"ב ס"ק יג. [116] סע' ח, מ"ב ס"ק מו, ס"ק מח בשם חיי"א, וע"ש בשעה"צ ס"ק צג. [117] ר' יונה בשם ר"ת ברכות ו/א בדפי הרי"ף ד"ה וכיוצא. [118] מ"ב ס"ק מו. [119] ס' תרמג סע' ג, שש"כ פמ"ח הע' מה. [120] מ"ב סק"ט. [121] מ"ב ס' תרלט סק"ל, שש"כ פנ"ח הע' קג, שו"ת שבט הלוי ח"ו ס' מב. [122] מ"ב ס"ק מח. [123] שם. [124] מ"ב ס"ק מז. [125] שם, פסקי תשובות הע' 74, גר"ז ס"ק יג. [126] ע' שעה"צ שם שנחלקו הפוסקים והפשרה שמעתי מאת הגר"צ ובר שליט"א מכיון שבלא"ה נחלקו הפוסקים אם מברך על מזונות. [127] שעה"צ ס"ק צא, וספק ברכות להקל. [128] גר"ז ס"ק יג. [129] שעה"צ ס"ק צד, מ"ב ס"ק מח. [130] ס' תרמ מ"ב סק"א. [131] מ"ב ס' תרמג סק"ד. [132] ס' תרמא סע' א. [133] ס' תרמג סע' א. [134] שם. [135] מ"ב סק"ג. [136] רמ"א ס' תרמא. [137] ס' תקסא, מ"ב סק"ב. [138] מ"ב ס' תעג סק"ג. [139] מ"ב סו"ס תרלט.

פרק י - גשם

[140] ס' תרלט סע' ה. [141] רמ"א שם. [142] ס' הסוכה השלם עמ' תכג סק"ב בשם א"א בוטשאטש. [143] מ"ב ס"ק לג. [144] שם. [145] רמ"א סע' ז. [146] דע"ת סע' ה, שבט הקהתי ח"א ס' קצט, ח"ג ס' קצב בשם הגריש"א. [147] סע' ז ברמ"א, מ"ב ס"ק מה. [148] רמ"א שם, משנה סוכה כח/ב, ערוה"ש סע' כ. [149] סע' ו, ז, מ"ב ס"ק לח, ביה"ל סוף הסימן. [150] מ"ב ס"ק מא. [151] שמעתי מהגר"צ ובר שליט"א, וע' מ"ב ס' כה ס"ק מז לעניין תפילין. [152] בסוכות תשבו פי"ג, ג (4) ובהע' 35. [153] מ"ב סו"ס תרלט. [154] רמ"א סו"ס תרכו, ס' שלו סע' ג, מ"ב ס"ק כז. [155] הל' שבת להגר"ש אידר עמ' 59 בשם הגרמ"פ, שש"כ פי"א הל' יח, הע' נא. [156] הגר"ש אידר שם הע' לו, כה"ח ס' שלו סע' כט. [157] ס' תרלט סע' ה ברמ"א, מ"ב ס"ק לה. [158] שם, שעה"צ ס"ק סז. [159] מ"ב ס"ק לו. [160] ס' רעג סע' א, ביה"ל ד"ה וכן. [161] מ"ב שם סק"כ, וביה"ל ד"ה והוא. [162] מ"ב ס' תרלט ס"ק לו, שעה"צ ס"ק סט, ס' קעח סע' ד,

מ״ב ס״ק מא. [163] מ״ב ס׳ תרלט שם. [164] שעה״צ
סק״ע. [165] מ״ב ס״ק לו.

פרק יא - מצטער פטור

[166] ס׳ תרמ סע׳ ג, ד, ז, ח. [167] רמ״א סוף סע׳ ד, מ״ס
סק״ל. [168] סע׳ ד, ביה״ל ד״ה מפני, ס׳ תרלט ס״ק לא, לב.
[169] מ״ב ס׳ תרמ ס״ק טז. [170] סע׳ ד ברמ״א, מ״ב ס״ק כג.
[171] ס׳ תרלט סע׳ ז ברמ״א וביה״ל, ספר סוכה השלם עמ׳
תכז. [172] ס׳ תרמ סע׳ ד. [173] מ״ב ס״ק כו. [174] רמ״א
סוף סע׳ ד, וע׳ מ״ב ס״ק לא. [175] מ״ב ס״ק טו. [176] סע׳
ג, מ״ב סק״ט. [177] מ״ב ס״ק ז, שעה״ת שם, ס׳ סוכה השלם
עמ׳ תכו. [178] מקור חיים (ח״י) סימן זה, ס׳ סוכה השלם
שם מסתפק בזה. [179] שבט הקהתי ח״ג ס׳ קצב אות ה.
[180] ביכור״י סק״ו. [181] סע׳ ז, ט, מ״ב ס״ק לה. [182]
מ״ב ס״ק לח, מו. [183] סוכה כהלכתה פרק י הע׳ כה.
[184] אוצר הברית פ״ד ס׳ י סק״א בשם הגריש״א, רמ״א ס׳
תרמ סע׳ ו. [185] מ״ב ס״ק לד, ביה״ל ד״ה וסעודת. [186]
אוצר הברית שם. [187] ביכור״י ס״ק כא, ביה״ל שם. [188]
סע׳ ח, מ״ב ס״ק לט, מ. [189] מ״ב ס״ק מא, מב. [190]
אג״מ ח״ג ס׳ צג, ספר סוכה השלם בשם הגרשז״א עמ׳ תנח.

פרק יב - כבוד הסוכה

[191] מ״ב ס׳ תרלט סק״ב, זוה״ק פ׳ אמור קג/ב. [192] ס׳
תרלט סע׳ א, ס׳ תרלח. [193] מ״ב ס׳ תרלט סק״ב, באה״ט
סק״ב. [194] מ״ב ס׳ תרלח סק״ד. [195] ס׳ תרלח סע׳ ב,
מ״ב סק״י. [196] ס״ק כד. [197] מ״ב ס״ק יג, יד. [198] ס׳
תרלח סע׳ ב ברמ״א, מ״ב ס״ק טו, ביה״ל ד״ה וביו״ט. [199]
ביה״ל ד״ה דמוקצים הם. [200] סע׳ ב, מ״ב ס״ק כג. [201]
שם. [202] מ״ב סק״כ. [203] ס׳ הסוכה השלם עמ׳ שעד
בשם דעת תורה ס׳ תרלח סע׳ ב ד״ה וע״ש. [204] מ״ב ס״ק
כד. [205] מ״ב ס״ק ט, כד, ביכור״י ס״ק יט. [206] גנזי
הקודש פי״ח הע׳ יד בשם הגר״נ קרליץ. [207] ס׳ תרלט סע׳
א. [208] מ״ב סק״ה, ט, ערוה״ש סק״ד. [209] מ״ב סק״ה.
[210] מ״ב סק״ו, שעה״צ ס״ק יג. [211] ערוה״ש סק״ג,
ביכור״י ס״ק יא. [212] שש״כ פכ״ח סע׳ עט, ארבעת המינים
כהלכתם בשם הגר״י זילברשטיין והגרח״ק. [213] ביכור״י

10. 'סק"י, ארחות רבינו ח"ב עמ' רכד, פסקי תשובות הע'
[214] מ"ב סק"ט.   [215] ערוה"ש סק"ד, קובץ בית דוד בשם
הגר"י זילברשטיין הובא בס' בסוכות תשבו פ"א סע' ה הע'
59.   [216] ע"פ הנ"ל.   [217] ערוה"ש הנ"ל.   [218] שם,
רבבות אפרים ח"א ס' תכא סק"ו יח בשם הגרמ"פ, שש"כ פכ"ד
סע' יג הע' מב*.   [219] פסקי תשובות אות ג בשם שו"ת לב
חיים.   [220] שם הע' 15 בשם הש"ך ועוד.   [221] זוה"ק פ'
אמור קג/ב, יסוד ושורש העבודה שער יא פי"ג, פלא יועץ ערך
סוכה.   [222] סוכה פ"ה, מ"ב סו"ס תרסא.   [223] ס' יו"ט שני
כהלכתו פ"ב סע' טו בשם הגרשז"א.

פרק יג - הימים האחרונים של סוכות

[224] ס' תרסו סע' א, מ"ב סק"ב.   [225] מ"ב סק"ט, ערוה"ש
סק"א.   [226] ס' תקסז ברמ"א, כה"ח סק"ז, וע' מ"ב ס' תעז
סק"ה.   [227] כה"ח שם.   [228] ס' תרסח סע' א, מ"ב סק"ו,
ערוה"ש סק"ג.   [229] מ"ב סק"ו, מעשה רב אות רכב, וע'
חיי"א כלל קנג סק"ה שהגר"א הקפיד מאד על זה.   [230]
שע"ת ס' תרסח ד"ה אוכלים, ס' יו"ט שני כהלכתו פ"ג סע' ל.
[231] ס' יו"ט שני כהלכתו פ"ב סע' יד בשם הגריש"א והגר"ש
ואזנר להחמיר, ושם בשם הגרשז"א, לוח א"י, מנח"י ח"ט ס'
נד, שש"כ פ' לא סע' מ' להקל.   [232] ס' תרסו סע' א.   [233]
שם.   [234] שם ומ"ב סק"ו.

פרק יד - הד' מינים

[235] ויקרא רבה פי' אמור פ' ל אות י"ב, סידור אוצר
התפילות עמ' 1176 בענף יוסף בשם מדרש אגדה.   [236] ע'
חיי אדם כלל קנא סע' ח שהמורים מרובים והיודעים
מועטים.   [237] ס' תרמט סע' ה.   [238] ח"א כלל קמט, סע'
ג, חיים וברכה אות סד.   [239] ח"א כלל קמח, סע' א.   [240]
ס' תרמט, מ"ב ס"ק לה.

פרק טו - אתרוג

[241] שו"ת חתם סופר ס' רז.   [242] ס' תרמט מ"ב ס"ק מה,
ס' תרמח ס"ק סה.   [243] פשוט.   [244] ס' תרמח סע' ב, ז, ט.
[245] ס' תרמח, מ"ב סק"ח, כד, כה, ביה"ל ד"ה ואם חסר.
[246] ס' תרמח סע' ו, מ"ב כד, כה, שעה"צ ס"ק כז, ויש
השיטות שאינו נקרא חסר עד שחסר כל קרום הירוק, הגר"ז

סע' טו, טז, ח"א כלל קנא סע' ה, חזו"א ס' קמז סק"א וסק"ה.
[247] מ"ב ס"ק יא. [248] שם סע' ח. [249] ס' תרמט סע'
ה, רמ"א ומ"ב סק"נ, ס' תרמח סק"ח, מקראי קודש ס' כו
באריכות בשם הראב"ד בתמים דעים ס' רלג והמאירי לו/ב.
[250] ס' תרמח סע' ז, וברמ"א. [251] שבולי הלקט ס' ש"ס,
קונטרס מבית לוי תשרי תשנ"ג עמ' כח סע' ו, יבקש תורה ס'
ח, הגר"י שוורץ בספרו ענף עץ עבות פ"ג ס"ק כד. וע' יבקש
תורה עמ' פא בשם החזו"א שאתרוג כזה הוי כשר לכתחילה.
[252] כה"ח אות מו, שפיטם דהוי בשר האתרוג נחשב חסר
אם נפל אפילו מקצתו, וכן סובר הגרש"ז אויירבעך הובא
במעדני שלמה עמ' צד, וכן הגריש"א שם בהערה מא. מ"ב
שם. [253] ס' תרמח מ"ב ס"ק לב. [254] ס' תרמח סע' ז
ברמ"א, מ"ב ס"ק לא. [255] ס' תרמט מ"ב ס"ק לו. [256] ס'
תרמח סע' טז, דעת תורה סע' טז, מ"ב ס"ק נה. [257] ס'
תרמח סע' יב, סע' י, מ"ב ס"ק מא. [258] סע' יב. [259]
ביה"ל ד"ה ממקום שמתחיל, חו"ב אות רנט. [260] מ"ב ס'
תרמח ס"ק מו. [261] ס' תרמט סע' ה ברמ"א, מ"ב ס"ק מט,
שעה"צ ס"ק נג. [262] שם ומ"ב ס"ק לח. [263] ע' ספר
כשרות ארבעת המינים להגרי"מ שטרן עמ' כא לגבי ריסוס.
[264] שם. [265] חזו"א סו"ס קמז. [266] חידושי חת"ס לו/א
ד"ה והנה, הכרעת הגר"ש וואזנר הובא בספר תורת ד' מינים
ס' כג סק"ל. [267] למנוע ממשמוש היד כל מה שאפשר.
[268] ס' תרמח סע' יג, מ"ב סק"נ, חיים וברכה אות סה, ח"א
כלל קנא, סע' ח. [269] רמ"א סע' ב. [270] סע' כב, שיעורין
של תורה שיעורי המצוות אות כה. [271] וחייב לפתוח
לפחות כל יום כדי למנוע ריקבון. [272] סו"ס תרמח, מ"ב
ס"ק סז, ס' תרנא סע' ב. [273] גר"ז סק"ל, מג"א ס"ק כג,
פרמ"ג א"א סו"ס תרמח. [274] סע' כא, מ"ב ריש ס"ק סה.
[275] חיים וברכה אות סה, סע' יח. [276] חיים וברכה שם.
[277] שם. [278] חיים וברכה שם, ס' תרנו סע א, ס' תרמח
מ"ב ס"ק לא.

פרק טז - לולב

[279] אע"פ דלא בעינן היתר אכילה, אבל יש פוסלים לולב
'קנרי' - ע' שו"ת אג"מ ח"ד ס' קכג. [280] ס' תרמ"ה, סע' א
ברמ"א, ומ"ב סק"ג. [281] מ"ב סק"ב. [282] סע' ג. [283]

שם. [284] שם וברמ"א. [285] שם. [286] מ"ב ס"ק טז, יט.
[287] שם. [288] מ"ב ס"ק טו. [289] מ"ב ס"ק טו. [290]
מ"ב ס"ק יט. [291] הגרי"י פישר בהסכמתו לספר ארבעת
המינים. [292] ס' תרמט סוס"ה, מ"ב ס' תרמה ס"ק יז.
[293] סע' ו, וביה"ל ד"ה רוב, עיקר הד"ט ס' לג אות כא , וכן
הורה החזו"א. [294] ביכור"י ס"ק טז, חיים וברכה אות רטז,
חזו"א ס' קמה סק"ה, ח, וע"ע כה"ח ס"ק מב, ס' ארבעת
המינים השלם עמ' רלט. [295] ביכור"י ס"ק טז, חיים וברכה
אות ריז, וע' מ"ב ס"ק כט. [296] ספר כשרות ארבעת המינים
להגרי"מ שטרן עמ' קנ. [297] מ"ב ס"ק כז. [298] כן משמע
בגר"ז סע' ט וכן אפשר לפרש דברי הארחות רבינו עמ' רלה.
דעה הב' ע"פ הגרש"ז אויירבעך הובא במעדני שלמה עמ' פא
ובספר ויאמר אברהם ס' תרמה סע' טז ס"ק כד. דעה הג' ע"פ
הגריש"א הובא במעדני שלמה שם הערה יא. [299] בספר
של הגרי"מ שטרן בשם הגריש"א, הגרשז"א הובא במעדני
שלמה עמ' פב. [300] סע' ז, מ"ב ס"ק לב, וע' מש"כ במעדני
שלמה עמ' פג בדעת המ"ב בזה. [301] מ"ב ס"ק לב. [302]
חיים וברכה אות קפג, ביכור"י ס' תרמט ס"ק לא. [303] ע'
מ"ב ס"ק טו לגבי נחלק (שפסולו משום לקיחה תמה) ונראה
דה"ה בפסול הימנק. וע' מ"ב ס"ק כט שנקטם א' אינו פסול,
ששם הפסול משום הדר, וע"ע בחזו"א ס' קמה סע' ה. [304]
חיים וברכה ס' קלח ע"פ הרמ"א ס' תרנא סע' ט. [305]
ארחות רבינו עמ' רלב/רלג דודאי כשר, אבל החזו"א
והסטייפלר עצמם הסירו הקורא לבדוק. [306] לחשוש לפי'
הריטב"א בפסול כווץ, וע' בספר ארבעת המינים להגרי"מ
שטרן, וע"ע בארחות רבינו עמ' רמד שהכשיר. [307] סע' ה,
מ"ב ס"ק כב, וע' חיים וברכה אות קג דלכתחילה נכון לחוש
שלא יהיה יבש כלל וכלל, אבל אינו פסול. וע"ע חזו"א ס'
קמה ס"ק י"א, ביה"ל סע' ז סד"ה נסדק בשם הר"ן. [308]
פשוט. [309] חזו"א שם, וע' במעדני שלמה עמ' פה ביאור
הדבר. [310] סע' ח ומ"ב ס"ק לג, חיים וברכה אות סו.
[311] שם ובמ"ב סק"מ, מ"א. [312] ס' תרמה מ"ב ס"ק מ,
מא, וע' ארחות רבינו עמ' רמו אות נ שכפוף למטה רק בקצה
לא מקרי כפוף, וע' במעדני שלמה עמ' פה. [313] ס' תרנ

סע' א, מ"ב סק"ח.   [314] חיים וברכה אות סו, ארחות רבינו
עמ' רמה אות מה, מג"א ס' תרעב סק"ג.

פרק יז - הדס

[315] מ"ב בהקדמה לס' תרמה.   [316] ס' תרנא סע' א.
[317] ס' תרמו סע' ג.   [318] ס' תרנ סע' א, ה, חזו"א ס' קמו
סק"ח.   [319] קהילת יעקב ס' כו בשם החזו"א.   [320] ס'
תרמו סע' ג.   [321] ביכור"י ס"ק יד.   [322] חיים וברכה אות
נט.   [323] סע' ה, ובמ"ב בביה"ל ד"ה ולעיכובא בס"ד.
[324] ביכור"י ס' תרמו ס"ק ד, דעת תורה ס' תרמז סע' ב.
[325] מג"א ס' תרמז סק"ב לגבי ערבה, ולפי הביכור"י ס' זה
סק"ד הדה"ה בהדס.   [326] מ"ב ס"ק לג, שעה"צ ס"ק לו.
[327] ס' תרמו סע' ו, ז, מ"ב ס"ק כ, לא.   [328] ס' תרמו סע' י
וברמ"א.   [329] פשוט.   [330] ס' תרנד סע' א.   [331] חיים
וברכה אות סז.

פרק יח - ערבה

[332] ס' תרמז סע' א.   [333] ס' תרנא סע' א.   [334] ס'
תרמז סע' א, הגרי"מ שטרן בשם הגרצ"פ פראנק.   [335] שם
ומ"ב סק"ב.   [336] כשרות ד' מינים להגרי"מ שטרן.   [337]
שם.   [338] מ"ב סק"ג.   [339] ס' תרנ סע' א.   [340] ס' תרמז
סע' ב, מ"ב ס"ק יא.   [341] דעת תורה ס' תרמז סע' ב.   [342]
מ"ב סק"ט.   [343] שעה"צ סק"ו, ארחות רבינו עמ' רנה אות
ה.   [344] סע' ב, ומ"ב ס"ק יב, סק"י.   [345] חיים וברכה אות
רמו.   [346] חיים וברכה אות סח, ס' תרנד ברמ"א.

פרק יט - קשירת המינים

[347] מ"ב סק"ז.   [348] ס' תרנ מ"ב סק"ח, ס' תרנא ס"ק יב.
[349] מ"ב ס"ק יב.   [350] ס' תרנא, סע' א.   [351] ס' תרנא
סע' א, גר"ז סע' י"א.   [352] ס' תרנא סע' א, חיים וברכה
אות רפח, מ"ב ס"ק ח, יד, חת"ס לו/ט ד"ה במינו, ביכורי יעקב
סק"ז, ח, ס' תרנד מ"ב סק"ה.   [353] ס' תרנ סע' א, ס' תרנא
סע' א.   [354] פשוט.   [355] ס' תרמט מ"ב ס"ק יד, שעה"צ
ס"ק טו.   [356] ס' תרנא סע' א ברמ"א.

פרק כ - נטילת המינים

[357] ס' תרנא מ"ב ס"ק לד, ס' תרנב סע' א ומ"ב סק"ד.
[358] ס' תרנא סע' ב, ה , מ"ב ס' תרנ סק"ח, חיי"א כלל קמח

[359] ס׳ תרנא סע׳ ג ברמ״א.   [360] מ״ב ס״ק יט, אות י.
שעה״צ ס״ק כג.   [361] ס׳ תרנא מ״ב ס״ק טו, חיים וברכה
אות קפז.   [362] ס׳ תרנא סע׳ ה, מ״ב ס״ק כד, סע׳ יא.
[363] מ״ב ס״ק כו.   [364] מ״ב ס״ק טז.   [365] ס׳ תרמד סע׳
א, מ״ב סק״ג.   [366] ס׳ תרמד מ״ב סק״ג, ס׳ תרנא ס״ק כט,
ביכור״י סק״כ.   [367] ס׳ תרנא סע׳ ה ברמ״א, ערוה״ש סע׳ יד.
[368] מ״ב ס״ק מז.   [369] שם.   [370] שם.   [371] מס׳ סוכה
לז/ב.   [372] ס׳ תרנא מ״ב ס״ק לז, ביכור״י ס״ק לו הובא
בשעה״צ ס״ק מט, כה״ח אות צו.   [373] ס׳ תרנא סע׳ ט
ברמ״א, מ״ב ס״ק מו.   [374] מקראי קודש ס׳ טז.   [375] ס׳
תרנא סע׳ ח, ס׳ תרס.   [376] ס׳ תרנא סע׳ יא, חיים וברכה
אות קפו.   [377] ס׳ תרנא סע׳ ח.   [378] מ״ב ס״ק לז, לט,
מא.   [379] מ״ב ס״ק מ״א.   [380] מ״ב ס״ק לז, כה״ח ס״ק פב.
[381] מ״ב ס״ק מ״א.   [382] סידור יעב״ץ דיני יום א׳ דסוכות
פ״ב אות י.   [383] ס׳ תרנח סע׳ א, ב, שש״כ פכ״ב, הע׳ נה.
[384] מ״ב סק״ב.   [385] ס׳ תרנא סע׳ ז, מ״ב ס״ק לו.   [386]
מ״ב שם.   [387] חיים וברכה אות צו, נשמת אברהם בשם
הגרשז״א, ערוה״ש סע׳ כ.

פרק כא - קניית המינים

[388] ס׳ תרנח סע׳ ג, מ״ב ס״ק כג.   [389] ס׳ תרמט סע׳ ב, ס׳
תרנח סע׳ ג, מ״ב ס״ק יא.   [390] מט״א ס׳ תרכה סע׳ יז, או״ש
פ״ח מהל׳ לולב ה״י.   [391] ס׳ תרנח סע׳ ו ביה״ל סד״ה לא
יתננו, מנח״י ח״ה ס׳ סה, ספר ארבעת המינים השלם עמ׳
תמח, תעה.   [392] ס׳ תרנח סע׳ ד.   [393] ס׳ תרנח שם ומ״ב
ס״ק יג.   [394] סע׳ ה.   [395] מ״ב ס״ק כא, כב, שעה״צ ס״ק
כו.   [396] מ״ב ס׳ תרנח ס״ק לט, חיים וברכה אות רצ בשם
ח״א, מבי״ט ועוד, וכן משמע במ״ב ס׳ תרמה ס״ק יח,
ובארחות רבינו עמ׳ רלא אות א.   [397] סע׳ ו, ביה״ל ד״ה
קודם שיצא.   [398] ס׳ תרנז מ״ב סק״ד, ביה״ל ס׳ תרעה ד״ה
ולדידן לגבי קטן בהידור מצוה, ס׳ תרנח רמ״א סוף סע׳ ט,
מ״ב ס״ק כח.   [399] ס׳ תרנז, שעה״צ סק״ב.   [400] ס׳ תרנח
סע׳ ט ברמ״א.   [401] ס׳ יז סע׳ ב מ״ב סק״ד.

פרק כב - הושענות

[402] משנה סוכה מה/א, רמב״ם פ״ז הל׳ לולב הל׳ כא, כב,
חיי״א כלל קמח סע׳ יט. [403] ס׳ תרס, מ״ב סק״ג . [404]
חיים וברכה אות קפו. [405] סע׳ ב ברמ״א. [406] מועד
לכל חי להגר״ח פלאג׳י ס׳ כג ס״ק ככ הובא בספר ארבעת
המינים השלם עמ׳ תנו. [407] סע׳ ב, שע״ת סק״א בשם
א״ר. [408] מ״ב סק״ד וסק״ו. [409] ס׳ תרסד סע׳ א, מ״ב
סק״ב, מנח״י ח״ח ס׳ פד סק״ב, מ״ב סק״א. [410] סע׳ א, מ״ב
סק״ב, פרמ״ג א״א ריש ס׳ תרסד. [411] ס׳ תרס סע׳ א
ברמ״א, ס׳ תרסד סע׳ א, וע׳ פרמ״ג מש״ז סק״א שמשאירים
טבעת אחת, ס׳ תרסד סע׳ א, ב. [412] ס׳ תרסד סע׳ ו, מ״ב
ס״ק כא. [413] מ״ב ס״ק טז. [414] סע׳ ג, לוח א״י. [415]
מ״ב ס״ק יז, ביכור״י ס״ק יא, ארחות רבינו ח״ב עמ׳
דש. [416] סע׳ ד, מ״ב ס״ק יב, ערוה״ש סק״ז. [417] ס׳ תרס
מ״ב סק״ח. [418] לוח א״י, ס׳ מועדי השנה להגרי״מ שטרן
[419] סע׳ ד, מ״ב ס״ק יט. [420] שו״ת דבר יהושע ח״ג ס׳
עד (ד), שבה״ל ח״ב ס׳ נח. [421] שו״ת מהרש״ם ח״ד ס׳ נז,
מועו״ז ח״ב ס׳ קלא בהג״ה אות ד, ס׳ תרסד סע׳ ט ברמ״א,
גר״ז ס׳ תמה סע׳ יב. [422] אלף המגן ס׳ תרס סע׳ ז, גר״ז ס׳
תמה סע׳ יב.

תם ונשלם שבח לה׳ בורא עולם

Shraga Feivel and
Rochel Leah King

Make this dedication
In honor of

Selig Osher
(Sheldon) King

devoted brother and
brother-in-law for his:

- Friendship
- Wisdom
- Love
- Support
- Compassion
- And unswerving
  dedication to the State of
  Israel.

May he live 120 years

In Loving memory of

Ken Gradon z"l

ר׳ יעקב ב״ר ברוך ז״ל

נלב״ע י״״ג סיון תשס״ב

Dedicated by
Mrs. Vera Gradon
and family

לע״נ

ר׳ שלמה ב״ר משה ז״ל

מרת רייזל דבורה בת
ר׳ יעקב מרדכי ע״ה

ר׳ יצחק ב״ר זאב ז״ל

לע"נ

ר' אברהם יצחק
ב"ר אליהו מענדל הכהן ז"ל

ואשתו מרת
פערל בת ר' שמעון לייב ע"ה

ת.נ.צ.ב.ה.

לע"נ

מרת פרידא
בת ר' שמעון הכהן ע"ה

ת.נ.צ.ב.ה.

לע"נ

מרת ביילא ע"ה
בת ר' לייב נ"י

ת.נ.צ.ב.ה.

לע״נ

Rebbetzin Miriam Greenblatt

**מרת מירל (מרים)
בת ר׳ אפרים נחמן ע״ה**

נפטרה חג השבועות תשס״ב

ת.נ.צ.ב.ה.

Dedicated to

Shulamit bat Faiza Aliza

*May Hashem send her a
Refuah Sh'leimah
and shower bountiful
blessings upon her*

לע"נ

הח׳ גד מאיר בן הר׳ יעקב ז"ל

ואשתו מרת ריזכא בת הר׳ גרשון ע"ה

ולע"נ

הח׳ משה בן ר׳ יעקב מיכאל ז"ל

ואשתו מרת שרה בת ר׳ יוסף ע"ה

ת.נ.צ.ב.ה.

Dedicated to our Children

Eli & Rivky Gordon
Shmuel & Chaya Gordon
Dovid & Rifky Ganz
and their children

May Hashem spread the shelter
of his peace over them
And over all the Jewish People

לע"נ

ר' יעקב ברוך
ב"ר איסר יצחק לי ז"ל

נלב"ע כ"ט מרחשון תשנ"ז

ת.נ.צ.ב.ה.

לע"נ

ר' צבי הירש בן ר' יעקב ז"ל

מרת שרה הניא בת
ר' אריה לייב הכהן ע"ה

ר' פינחס משה בן
ר' דניאל הכהן ז"ל

Mr. Tuvia Gitt z"l

Mr. Sam Zemmel z"l

ת.נ.צ.ב.ה.

Dedicated to the memory of

Dr. Moshe Ze'ev Gottleib z"l

who was tragically killed,

and to his bereaved family.

May Hashem comfort
and console them
and avenge the
blood of the innocent.

ת. נ. צ. ב. ה.

From the Steinberg,
Smith & Boxer Families